ELDER WISDOM

ELDER WISDOM

Searching for Truth in Circles of Women

ANITA McLEOD

ELDER WISDOM
Searching for Truth in Circles of Women

Designed by Bonnie Campbell

Printed in the United States of America
ISBN: 978-0-9960826-8-6
Library of Congress Control Number: 2019953815

Copies of this book may be ordered from:
RCWMS
1202 Watts Street
Durham, NC 27701
www.rcwms.org
info@rcwms.org

TABLE OF CONTENTS

FOREWORD

~~~~~~

MY DEAR FRIEND Anita McLeod was a most unusual woman. Raised in New Jersey as the daughter of Norwegian immigrants, Anita lived her adult life in Durham, North Carolina, where she loved and explored life as a wife, mother, grandmother, friend, nurse, health educator, retreat leader, and more. Among her most important explorations with her husband, Mike McLeod, and with friends and family, were sailing, dancing, hiking, camping, sewing, spirituality, yoga, and drumming. These may not sound like unusual interests, but Anita did not take on these roles and activities in traditional ways. Filled with wonder and searching for beauty always, she was an Earth-Lover, Water-Protector, Gatherer of Circles, Planter and Gleaner of Wisdom, and Feminist Elder. Even in her last weeks of life, facing tremendous physical limitations and challenges brought on suddenly by a brain tumor, Anita McLeod continued to embody Wild Girl, Wondering Mother/Lover, and Mystic Crone.

This small volume is a collection of writings by and about Anita McLeod, published with the hope of savoring and sharing her wisdom and joy. The book is divided into two parts: The first three sections are comprised of Anita's own writing from 2003 to 2016; the last section includes words written and spoken about Anita after her death, including her obituary. Arranged in a mostly chronological manner to show how her interests and insights developed over time, the pieces broadly reflect Anita's intertwined commitments to feminism, conscious aging, and the natural world.

Anita began writing for others in 2003, largely as a result of her rich connection to the Resource Center for Women and Ministry in the South (RCWMS or the Resource Center), which for nearly twenty-five years provided a container and incubator for Anita's explorations. Anita contributed regularly to the Resource Center newsletter, *South of the Garden*, and eventually began writing specifically for the RCWMS Elder Women's Spirituality Project. These writings reflect Anita's pursuit of wisdom in her sixties and seventies, what Mike McLeod has described as her "courage to live her questions." Her collaborations with the Resource Center and with its founder and executive director, Jeanette Stokes, gave Anita a platform for exploring her questions in community.

In her writings, you will find only a portion of Anita McLeod's wisdom because she was a rather reluctant public writer. As a feminist, Anita preferred to find knowledge and meaning in experience and in communal reflection. Anita believed in her body and the wisdom we can access from our own flesh and spirit. Although her workshops seemed to flow in an organic way, Anita prepared for weeks, drawing on her strong capacities to organize material and synthesize literature on health and spirituality. For her, workshops and retreats were not forums to tell us what she knew about menopause, or being a woman over sixty, or how to love Earth and Her waters. Workshops were opportunities to learn and experience with others. Notice in her writing how Anita so frequently explains the foundation for her projects: "I wanted to learn, to have meaningful conversations, and to contemplate my choices in a circle of thoughtful women." In her workshops about and for women in their last third of life, participants harvested their own wisdom in order to find meaning and new possibilities.

What may not be apparent from these readings alone is the courage that Anita brought to her work with the Resource Center, the courage to "live her questions." Anita led workshops and wrote about the dimensions of life that most frightened her. She had been taught in her childhood to "simmer down" and not "show off," but as an adult Anita wrangled unwieldy ideas and uncertain women into sacred circles and supported them to be expressive and extravagant in their desires and dreams and pursuit of beauty. Anita was wary of pain and illness, but she chose a career as a nurse and health educator. She was highly empathic and could be overwhelmed by intense emotion in others, and yet she created safe spaces for those feelings and invited women to share from their deepest selves. Anita was terrified of aging and the grief and loss that can accompany diminishing physical capacity and social relevance, but she walked into these fears with fierce compassion for herself and for those who journeyed with her.

In the second part of this book—in thoughts shared

about Anita by her husband, Mike, and family and friends—
you will learn a great deal about who Anita McLeod was in
her communal and familial connections. You will learn a bit
about how others experienced her and her presence in the
world. These are not the only stories. There are other stories
of Anita from people, especially women, who had deep relationships with her and who were profoundly touched by
her presence in their lives. Anita maintained and nurtured
friendships with women from all stages of her life, from
girlhood through her seventies. They loved and admired her
deeply, and new friends and old helped Anita create wisdom
and joy and share it with the world around her.

Friendship with Anita could be life-changing. I met her
in 1998 when RCWMS helped facilitate a year-long course
on feminist spirituality at Duke Divinity School. Perhaps
like others, I can remember exactly where I was in my first
conversation with Anita. At the time, perched with her on
a sofa at Duke, I thought I saw a large light blinking ex-
citedly above Anita's head, telling me, "Pay attention! This
woman is special! She is extraordinary!" Over the following
years, Anita and I saw one another at workshops and events.
In 2006, we began hiking together as a kind of therapy to
cope with the losses of each of our brothers. We would meet
in the woods once or twice a week. Occasionally we would
chat about our children, grandchildren, husbands, and dogs.
Usually, however, we came to the woods together to engage
in something much deeper: Our questions for one another
were, "How goes it with your Soul?" and "How does this

Forest sustain you today?" Anita was one of the few people I could be completely silent with for hours on end, deeply present and without pretense. Our walking and talking expanded to camping in North Carolina and Virginia, from the coast to the mountains, where we would sit, silently, and experience the "great slowing" that comes with conspiring (breathing together) with the water and trees. Mike and others know well the experience I am describing. Being in the natural world with Anita was like living a Mary Oliver poem.

When I was treated for cancer in 2009, Anita committed to making the journey with me and with my family. Given her empathic distress around hospitals, illness, and death, I was honored and comforted by her presence at medical appointments. In the day-to-day experiences of major medical treatment, Anita turned the fearful and mundane into beauty. In the old Gravely Hospital at the University of North Carolina, chemotherapy patients and their companions often sat in close, cramped rooms with multiple infusions happening at once. On several occasions, I would fall asleep during my infusion and awaken to find Anita alive, engaged, and present with the others in the room. Once I opened my eyes to see that a handsome twenty-year-old man had come in for treatment. His cancer was obviously a very serious one, and his mother cared for him as best she could. I expected Anita to be in pain at this sight, both of us imagining our own beloved children, but that was not the case. Her eyes were shining, and she said later she could actually see the love glowing between the boy and his mother. As my illness and treatment progressed over the summer, I found myself too weak to go to the woods. Anita knew there was nothing sadder for me than the fear that I might not hike again. So, she went to the woods and called me on her cell phone. As she walked, she described blossoms and rocks, singing birds and sunning turtles. One day, Anita stood before a great tree and told me about the grooves in her bark, her roots and branches, the shape and color of the leaves and how they quivered in the breeze. She whispered a prayer, "Behold this tree. Behold this tree." On my bed, tears soaking the pillow, ear to the phone, I found I could indeed behold the tree beside her.

This book provides a glimpse of the ways that Anita McLeod touched her family and community, reminding us of Earth's beauty and capacity to accept our suffering and heal us, if only we will ask and be present with courage.

When you have read this book, I invite you to set these pages aside, and *DO what Anita would do:* Go out into the woods and experience the earth under your feet and the leaves rustling near you. Touch your Beloved and actually feel the magic of their skin on your skin. Take your own pulse and ask your body what it needs you to know. Take your place in a circle of women, and be present to the knowledge you can create together if you are willing to let go of persona and journey deep enough. Imagine and trust the possibilities of wisdom, beauty, and joy that danced in the life of Anita McLeod.

—*Barbara Shaw Anderson*
CARRBORO, NC

INTRODUCTION

AFTER ANITA DIED on January 9, 2017, after her memorial service on January 16, and after a period of intense grief, what set in was a profound sense of what we had lost. At her husband Mike's suggestion, we began to collect the written record of Anita's work with the Resource Center and some of her other reflections on life. That is what you hold in your hands. It is divided into four sections, beginning with a collection of Anita's writings for *South of the Garden,* the RCWMS quarterly newsletter. Now in its fortieth year, the newsletter includes calendar listings and program information as well as essays on a wide variety of topics. Anita had a particular gift for incorporating her own insights into her journey through life's passages. These learnings form the basis for her Elder Women reflections that constitute the second section of this book. Other Writings, the third section, illustrates some of Anita's varied interests as she reflects on the phases of a woman's life, conscious aging, nature, friends she had lost, and the promise of a couple's new marriage. The book concludes with words about Anita from beloved family and friends. We still miss her, and hope these words bring you solace and inspiration for the journey ahead.

Jeanette Stokes
Executive Director, RCWMS

SECTION I

RCWMS NEWSLETTER ARTICLES

ANITA WROTE FOR *South of the Garden* beginning in 2003. She also developed, convened, co-led, and participated in many workshops over the years. Those workshops are listed in Appendix B. We have included the original dates for the written pieces and for the workshop to illustrate the evolution of Anita's work.

MENOPAUSE

December 2003 · Vol. 24, No. 4

Menopause is a powerful mystery. It can be a deeply meaningful spiritual and psychological transition, the threshold for what is possibly the most powerful stage in a woman's life.

I didn't know this in 1989 when I went to the gynecologist about my irregular menstrual cycles. I wasn't experiencing hot flashes or sleep difficulties yet. I thought I might be entering menopause and just wanted to rule out disease. I was healthy and had recently reduced my elevated cholesterol by fifty points with exercise and diet. I was hoping for an acknowledgement of my efforts.

My doctor agreed I was menopausal and then proceeded to explain all the reasons he thought I should take hormone replacement therapy (HRT). I listened. I had intuitively felt that HRT was not for me. I had avoided birth control pills when they were first available because I was concerned about the side effects. I believed my body knew how to be healthy as long as I exercised, ate well and addressed my stress. I told the doctor my concerns about HRT and that I would not be following his advice for now. His irritated reply was, "Want to arm wrestle over it?" I was outraged by his power play and left his office determined to learn as much as I could about healthy menopause.

I began attending lectures by physicians and reading medical literature, which were depressing. They put a "disease spin" on a normal life transition. All the talk about disintegration, deterioration, and future complications "awfulized" the changes and scared women. The emphasis was on disease and drugs, not on opportunities for creating a healthy and vibrant life. So I began making my own way through the midlife transition, reading everything supportive I could find, which at that time was limited to books by Rosetta Reitz and Sadja Greenwood. I learned that the transition of menopause occurs normally in a woman's late forties or early fifties, except when brought on by hysterectomy. Four out of five women experience hot flashes and night sweats, but the frequency, intensity, and duration vary widely. The flashes are usually the most intense for the first two years and decrease as the body adapts to lower hormone levels and finds a new equilibrium. Flashes can be set off by emotional upset and stress, hot food and drink, alcohol and caffeine, hot weather and hot rooms. Exercise and relaxation can reduce the intensity and frequency of hot flashes. HRT can be a temporary solution for women whose quality of life is compromised by sleeplessness and resulting depression.

I decided another way to learn about menopause was to offer workshops on healthy menopause. The workshops gave me a chance to listen to hundreds of women speak of their own experiences. What I learned reinforced what I was reading in books by feminist authors, that we did not have to be helpless and hopeless victims of our hormones, that we can take action on our own behalf.

While the menopause journey can be about empowerment and self-care, most of us begin in a place of fear. Woman after woman said her body felt out of control. As we told our stories, we discovered we were not alone, which greatly reduced our fear and stress. In listening to ways others found to cope with their hot flashes and sleep difficulties, we found creative ways to cope with our own changes. To cool down, women carried fans to work, put cold cloths on their necks, or walked outside on a cold night. When awake in the night some made tea and read poetry or listened to peaceful music. Others turned an extra room into a late-night sanctuary.

In group after group, women arrived tense and anxious and left relieved that they were not alone in their experience. The support of a community of women has a huge potential for healing. Many women said they wanted time for themselves but felt that was selfish. We reminded one other that our lives are our own and we are responsible to ourselves for our choices. We remembered that, as with many transitions, discomfort is temporary and can wake us up to our inner voices and desires.

Our culture has such a negative image of menopause. Middle-aged women are portrayed as emotional wrecks, drenched in sweat, and unable to cope with life's stress. We are told we have much to lose at menopause. In fact, the changes are disruptive, but we have much to gain if we listen to our inner wisdom and follow its guidance. All kinds of things happen. Some women get cranky and are proud of it. Some make time to exercise, meditate, paint, or write. Others go back to school, change careers, become poets or vegetarian chefs. Responding to menopause as an invitation to turn inward can bring rich gifts from our inner wellspring. For me, the joy of dancing, the discovery of the Divine Feminine, and the rediscovery of the sacred in the natural world are treasures from my midlife journey.

During puberty, our cascading female hormones change our bodies, feelings, perceptions, and our sense of self. Menopause can be viewed as a mirror image of puberty when shifting hormones lead to changes that bring us back to our authentic self. Just as a girl is transformed into a woman by the mystery of her sacred biology, a midlife woman can be changed by the experience of menopause. By responding with compassion to her body and psyche she begins to nurture herself and then has more to share with the world.

After years of listening and caring for others, it is time

to listen and care for ourselves, to compost our life experiences into wisdom that will guide us through the rest of our lives. Following our heart's wisdom can be the path through this dynamic journey of transformation.

OVER 60

~~~~~~~~~~~~~~~~~~~~~~~~~

April 2005 • Vol. 26, No. 1

It is a cold morning in March and I am sitting on a hard, grey metal folding chair in the large parlor of a funeral home in northern New Jersey. There are no windows in the dimly lit room. The pale blue walls and rose carpet soften the sounds of people whispering and weeping. Colorful sprays of mums, roses, and lilies surround the satin-lined open casket holding the body of my only sibling, my brother Paul. He was only sixty-one years old when he suffered a massive heart attack and died instantly at his home. I am overwhelmed with grief and loss and shock. No chance for goodbyes. I am now the sole survivor of my family of origin.

As the tears roll down my flushed face, I look around the parlor for familiar faces and realize all the elders—my aunts, uncles and parents—are not here. They have passed on. All of them. Tante Solveig, Uncle Anton, Tante Astrid, Uncle Oscar, Tante Esther and Uncle Conrad, as well as my parents, Catherine and Arne Swensen. A whole generation is gone. All the old folks are dead. They had always held up the sky for us children. Now my two cousins, Greta and Anton, and I are the elders. We are the old people. I feel not only the loss of my brother, but also the loss of my family and my youth. How did this happen so quickly? I am 65 years old and there is no one between death and me. I have been pondering many questions about aging since I became 60, and Paul's death jolts me, bringing a sharp focus to my quest.

Entering my sixties has felt like walking into a strange new territory. I have crossed the threshold of middle age into a new land without a map or a guide. What does it mean to be an elder? How do I stay conscious in this new land? What is my soul's gift to the community? How do I restore and rejuvenate myself so that my voice and actions are authentic? I know I cannot do this alone. I know that I am closer to death than I have ever been.

In April 2004, RCWMS sponsored a workshop, "Women Over Sixty." I created the workshop because I wanted to have meaningful conversations with women near my age who might be asking questions like mine. During the course of the day we shared our sense of physical vulnerability and our strong desire for health and independence. Some of us spoke about our freedom from caretaking, while others had new responsibilities caring for elderly parents or grandchildren. We considered our feelings about how we use time. Most of us said we wanted more quiet time for prayer, contemplation, and reflection. We shared our vulnerabilities, our strengths and our yearnings. We also began the process of harvesting wisdom, collecting what we have learned from our life experiences that we can pass on to others.

For several years, I have been asking myself a version of

Mary Oliver's question from her poem "The Summer Day," what is it I want to do with the rest of my one wild and precious life?[1] I now realize that before I can answer that question, I need to accept that I am mortal and will die one day. This is not a new thought, it just feels more real since my brother's death. I want to be connected to my soul when I die, and even more than that, I want to be connected to myself while I live. This is my journey now: To deepen my relationship to my soul and carry my soul with me into each day. To do that, I need solitude and a community where it is safe for soul to show up and speak, as Parker Palmer discusses in *A Hidden Wholeness*. I am grateful to the women of RCWMS who provide a community for me and a container in which to explore these soulful issues.

SNAKE

December 2007 • Vol. 28, No. 4

Returning home from my women's group on a hot summer night this year, I drove into my driveway and noticed how dark the front of the house looked. The porch light was off and only the soft glow of a gaslight in the yard penetrated the darkness. I jumped out of my car and hurried up the short walkway through shrubbery and dense groundcover to the porch. "Ouch!" I screamed, as I felt a sudden piercing pain in my right foot just below the anklebone. It felt like something bit me.

I ran up the steps to the porch, put the key in the lock, and opened the front door. As I walked inside, the pain increased. "I think I have been bitten by a snake," I said to the house and to my husband who was reading in a blue chair by the fireplace. By the time I reached the couch across the room from him, I could hardly put weight on my right leg. "Oweee, it really hurts," I howled as I lay down, shoving two cushions under my throbbing lower leg.

"It couldn't be a snake, it must be a bee sting," my husband offered. "I have been stung by bees and wasps, and this is not a sting. It hurts a lot more," I insisted. I looked down at my foot and saw two closely spaced blood red spots just in front of my anklebone. I was sure I had been bitten by a snake. I knew immediately that I did not want to go to the Emergency Room because I did not want crisis medical management. I did not feel I was in crisis. Quite the opposite, I felt a strange sense of calm and was sure I would be okay. Instead of being poisoned, perhaps I had been marked.

I did not have a bad reaction to the snake venom. My lower leg and ankle swelled and bruised, but there were no signs of severe inflammation requiring medical treatment. We applied some pressure to limit the spread of venom and I kept my foot propped up all night. A physician friend of ours who had worked with snakebites in Africa came by for a look and confirmed that I had definitely been bitten by a snake, most likely a good-sized copperhead, and that my body was handling it well.

He did not suggest any further treatment and saved our family beach vacation by recommending I wear a compression stocking so I could walk. While my leg healed in a week, I sensed that I would be exploring the symbolic meaning of being marked by a snake for years to come.

About twelve years ago, I found a beautiful whole snakeskin on the same front walkway. That particular day, I was coming home in the late afternoon from teaching one of my first classes on menopause. As I listened to the women speak of the mystery of their menopausal experiences, chills ran up and down my body and I knew it to be an extraordinary moment. When I found the snakeskin on my front walk, I took it to be a sign of a turning point, not unlike menopause. I carefully gathered it up and placed it in my medicine bag. I continued to lead menopause classes for another ten years, encouraging women to listen to their bodies, to trust and speak of their own experiences and to explore the mystery of this major life transition.

Being bitten by the snake may be a sign at another turning point in my life. My ninety-three-year-old mother-in-law died the week before the bite. She was a strong Southern woman who had lived independently for most of her life with fierceness, grace, and a deep faith that served her well. She died a peaceful death surrounded by three generations of family who loved and respected her. She showed me it is possible to die to this world, to leave all that you love, to let go and move on in peace. She had been a teacher for me in life and now in death she gave a powerful teaching to me and to all her family. Many of my dearest women friends showed up for her memorial service. Most had not met my mother-in-law: they were there because they loved me. Twenty-five years ago when my parents died and two years ago when my brother died, few of my friends could attend their services because they took place out of state. I now know what I missed.

At my mother-in-law's funeral, a friend said to me, "Now you are the matriarch of the family, you are the female elder." I understand the snakebite as an initiation to my elder years, and a calling to gather older women together in circles to explore elderhood and conscious aging.

I want to sit in sacred circles with women who are excavating the meaning of their lives and are willing to explore the terrain of getting older. I want women to wake up and define for themselves what holds power and value for them in the years beyond fifty. I want women to recognize the sacred moments that are happening in their everyday lives. I dream of groups of older women mentoring and supporting younger women as they learn to honor the wisdom of their bodies and choose to follow the sacred threads of their life experience. I long for the companionship of wise elders and that is why I offer workshops and retreats.

I've long known that I experience the presence of the Holy when I am in nature and with people I care about. I now understand aging as a spiritual journey that can be nourished and deepened sitting in a circle of women. The snake helped remind me that life is precious and finite and it is time for me to pay close attention to how and where I spend my life energy.

CIRCLES

December 2009 • Vol. 30, No. 4

I invited thirty women to my home one evening in November 2009, to help me celebrate turning seventy. Most of the women who came were members of the various women's circles to which I belong. There were women I worked with at Duke Hospital twenty years ago. The wild women circle that began after a class on Exploring Women's Spirituality has been meeting monthly for fifteen years. Another circle grew out of a yearlong Duke Divinity School class on women and spirituality twelve years ago. There were women who were on the RCWMS Board of Trustees with me, yet another circle. The youngest woman present taught a water aerobics class at the YMCA, a circle in deep water. Other circles present included a yoga circle, a sailing circle, a circle from a weekend party, an elder circle that grew out of a "Women Over Sixty" workshop sponsored by RCWMS, and a "Crow Women" circle that grew out of a January writing week at Trinity Center. As we came together in a new, larger circle, we discovered that many of us knew one another from

RCWMS events such as "Art and the Feminine Divine," the Meinrad Craighead Documentary Project, Wise Choices retreats, and writing workshops. RCWMS itself is a huge circle out of which many other circles are spawned. Women who want to be in community naturally form circles of meaning and purpose. Many women choose to live their lives within overlapping and interconnected circles.

Some circles meet around a table and share food and life stories. Some form to plan and carry out a project. Others create ritual and ceremony. Still others gather in silence around a candle for meditation and deep reflection. Circles help us create, help us get our work done, and give us a safe home in which to be our full selves. Within a structured format, circles encourage us to speak the truth, to listen deeply, and to hold each other in unconditional positive regard. There are helpful guidelines for creating, sustaining, and maintaining safe circles. A strong circle is based on a covenant and agreements the members make with one another. In an egalitarian structure, the participants hold the rim of the circle while the center contains the sacred energy where souls can touch.

The feminine divine is at work in the center of such circles calling us to our deepest and most authentic selves, mending the places of conflict and brokenness, and calling forth healing. She calls us to be together in community, to be at home in our world.

In October, I attended Crones Counsel at a retreat center near Atlanta. Over 150 women, ages fifty to ninety-five, came from twenty-five states, many of them traveling from the West Coast where Crones Counsel began. They gathered to celebrate and cherish their aliveness and deepen their wisdom. Four days of storytelling, workshops, dancing and drumming, sacred ceremony, and honoring the elders engraved my soul with sparkling images of aging women, fiercely alive.

I got excited about turning seventy, about becoming even more free and expressive. I saw that getting old did not mean I had to be quiet or compliant. I can be myself, wild and free. Participants met with the same small group for sharing each day. In my circle, I met elders whose openness, humor, sexuality, and courage contradicted all the cultural stereotypes of "old women." Being in circle with these wise elders inspired me to offer more workshops on women's circles and on eldering.

At my birthday celebration, there were gifts of music and singing, poetry and art, skits, stories, and ceremony. I felt initiated, mirrored, celebrated, honored, and deeply loved. The gratitude and love I feel I will carry to other circles of family and community. The depth of our presence with one another reflects our having learned to share our hearts with each other in a circle. I wish every woman could have such a powerful rite of passage at a significant time in her life.

The circle is an ancient symbol of wholeness, a form whose time has come again. Thousands of years of hierarchical, patriarchal leadership has endangered our planet and led to inequality and chaos among people. It is time to strengthen the circle model in our families and in our communities as we work and play together to heal our earth and all our relations.

ELDER WOMEN'S NETWORK: CONNECTING CIRCLES OF WOMEN

December 2010 · Vol. 31, No. 4

More women are entering their sixties, seventies, and eighties with better health, higher levels of education, greater work experience, and more resources than ever before. We have choices our mothers and grandmothers never dreamed of, and we can now ask, as poet Mary Oliver asks in her poem "The Summer Day," *What is it you plan to do with your one wild and precious life?*[2] Each of us was born with a gift for the world, and as we grow older, the desire to share that gift grows more urgent.

The women of the feminist movement of the 1960s and '70s are now elder women. We have lived purposeful lives and want meaningful action to continue to be our central concern, but we don't want to go to more meetings or form new organizations. We want to focus our energy, joining together in community to lend our voices and actions to what we love and value.

Elder women are expressing deep concern for future generations and deep dismay over the declining health of our planet. Women who were inspired and changed by the feminist movement are leading the way, and many are looking to the indigenous women of the world for wisdom and guidance. The archetype of the powerful wise old woman, which has been all too absent from the western world, is now rising in the land. My hope is that women will find community and support for their spiritual journeys as they work on behalf of their deepest concerns.

In the past twenty years, I have facilitated circles of women exploring healthy menopause, midlife issues, being over sixty, and creating soulful circles of support. Now, at the age of seventy, I want to connect these pieces. I am creating the Elder Women's Network as a project of RCWMS in order to offer women opportunities to bring the wisdom of their experience forward and join with others in having a positive impact on our world.

My goal is to inspire elder women to be a force for peace and justice, especially in North Carolina. Many elder women already contribute to local community organizations. An Elder Women's Network would encourage them further by linking them to other women doing similar work. Participating women can form small groups for action and reflection, and the groups can be connected to one another through RCWMS. My hope is that women will find community and support for their spiritual journeys as they work on behalf of their deepest concerns.

The Elder Women's Network sponsored several events in 2010—two gatherings in October and several film showings. "When the Grandmothers Speak, the Earth Will Heal" was a day-long retreat at The Center for Education, Imagination, and the Natural World at Timberlake Farms near Greensboro, North Carolina (www.beholdnature.org). On a beautiful October morning, twenty-six women gathered in a circle in the sundrenched living room of the farmhouse. Carolyn Toben and her staff led us through a morning of meditations, shared stories, and silent walks to affirm our personal connections to the earth. We ate an organic lunch outside on the porch with dappled sunlight shining through the trees. Many of us remembered being free to discover the forests, rivers, and creeks of our childhood, finding solace and delight in the natural world. Since so many children today lack this intimate bond with the natural world, we explored ways to share our love for the earth with children. As we listened to the deep sounds of the woodlands with "the ears of a deer," many of us vowed to share this experience with the children in our lives.

Two weeks later, thirteen women came to my home to hear about the Nyanya Project (www.nyanyaproject.org) from Bett Hargrave, a grandmother and former RCWMS board chair. Bett traveled to Kenya in 2009 with her three grown daughters to visit the project, which offers hope and support to African grandmothers who are raising their AIDS-orphaned grandchildren. Mary Martin Niepold, a journalism professor at Wake Forest University, started the project. While volunteering with children orphaned by AIDS in Kenya in 2006, Mary, a grandmother herself, asked, "Who is helping the grandmothers?" No one was. Grandmothers are raising over a million orphans in Kenya alone. These women, who receive no government aid, manage to support families of ten or more on as little as a dollar a day.

Mary used her own funds and contributions from friends to begin the Nyanya Project. When she asked the grandmothers what they needed, they said their grandchildren needed a preschool, so Nyanya helped build the school. Bett visited the first preschool in 2009 and returned home to form a grandmother circle in her hometown of Lexington, NC, and raise money for ongoing support. A second preschool opened in 2010. The women at my house were so inspired by what we heard that we made contributions to the project and began to think about forming our own giving circles.

The Elder Women's Network has sponsored several showings of *For the Next 7 Generations* this year. The film features the International Council of Thirteen Indigenous Grandmothers, wise elders who teach us that we are connected to each other and to all living beings on the earth. My hope is that elder women who see the film will join in conversation afterward and be inspired to create circles of their own focused on common concerns. The support of like-minded women can empower women in these groups to take action on behalf of what they love.

END OF LIFE SERIES: CONTEMPLATING DEATH, EMBRACING LIFE

December 2011 • Vol. 32, No. 4

To be blessed in life, one must learn to die.
To be blessed in death, one must learn to live.

—PHILIPPE DUPLESSIS-MORNAY,
   Mémoires Et Correspondance

Entering the decade of my 70s has inspired me to reexamine the end-of-life decisions I made in my 50s and 60s. I am now deeply motivated to learn more about current end-of-life options and contemplate my choices in a circle of thoughtful women. I do not want to do this alone. I have learned so much about living into my elder years by participating in a variety of women's circles over the past twenty years. Hearing the experiences and stories of others has always inspired and deepened my own process. At a "Wise Choices" retreat several years ago a woman said, "I am here to consider what will comfort me when I am dying." Her brave words touched a deep place in my heart and I continue to learn from reflecting on her question. It is my contemplation of her question that led me to put together a workshop series on end-of-life issues, which RCWMS will offer in 2012.

Death is a taboo topic in our culture. There are very few times and places we talk with others about our own death. Every one of us is going to die, yet we act as if death will not happen to us. We plan for so many things during our lifetime, yet we often fail to make plans for the end of our life. People end up in situations they would never choose for themselves, such as dying in a hospital rather than at home because they had not made their wishes known. Many of us do not want to inadvertently end up spending our last days on earth hooked up to a breathing machine, being fed through a feeding tube, and having extravagant painful procedures performed on us, all because we did not complete a plan for the health care we want at the end of our life. The idea of considering our preferences in a circle of others willing to explore these issues has led me to invite three skilled and empathic professional women to join me in leading this series.

In one session, we will reflect on our experiences with death and dying. As we write and speak and listen, we become more aware of our hopes and wishes regarding our own death. We will learn more about what we want, identify how we want to be treated, and be fortified to have meaningful conversations with our loved ones.

During another session, we will discuss the essential legal documents needed to protect yourself, your health and your assets. These documents include healthcare powers of attorney, living wills, powers of attorney, and wills and trusts. We will consider the legal implications of these documents and how they can be used to ensure that your wishes will be carried out. In addition, there will be time to consider how these documents might bring up sensitive family issues and how to address them with your loved ones.

In another session, we will explore what a "good death" might look like and what possibilities are available to help us achieve our ideal dying experience. This exploration will include contemplating individual spiritual views, and how secular and religious traditions may have shaped us in ways inconsistent with those spiritual views.

The purpose of this series is to prepare as consciously and compassionately as we can for our own death, so we can live fully in the present. What are the essential conversations, documents, and desires we want to have so we can "let go" and live more fully in our current life? We may consider how we want to say "goodbye" and what is the legacy we wish to leave our family and community. We can then cherish the precious time remaining to us by wholeheartedly embracing the future that beckons us.

ELDERS

September 2012 • Vol. 33, No. 3

People ask me if the Elder Women's Spirituality Project is about providing care and services for elderly women. This puzzled me until I realized there is not a clear distinction between elderly and elder. Elderly implies fragility or impairment requiring assistance. Elder refers to a person of age who is still growing, learning, and engaged in action. It is a term of respect, implying wisdom gained from lived experiences.

We live in a culture that worships youthfulness and fears aging. We need to bring the wise elder woman (or crone) back into our culture, because she can translate wisdom from her own life into a legacy for future generations. Our society needs grandmothers who know the earth is alive and sacred and who love the children of all beings.

The Elder Women project offers workshops that nurture and strengthen elder women. Join us for one of our programs this fall. "Harvesting Our Stories: Collecting Our Wisdom," a writing workshop, will help us cull through our lived experiences to find pearls of wisdom we can translate into a legacy for future generations. "When the Grandmothers Speak, the Earth will Heal" will help us imagine ways to share our love of the earth with the children in our lives. "Giving Thanks to the Earth" will deepen our connection to the natural world through basic movement, writing, music, simple drawing, and time outdoors.

ELDER WOMEN

December 2012 • Vol. 33, No. 4

What a year this has been for the Elder Women's Project! A $20,000 grant from the Kalliopeia Foundation jumpstarted our programs and gave energy to our efforts. Approaching the end of 2012, I find myself reflecting on our programmatic emphasis on the sacred in the natural world and its vital importance for us and our planet. This came home to me in October when Ann Koppelman led an experiential workshop, "Giving Thanks to the Earth," which used movement, simple art projects, music, and quiet time in nature to awaken and deepen our connection with the earth.

My experience in Ann's workshop led me to ask Carolyn Toben, an educator and spiritual teacher, to give a reading from her beautiful new book, *Recovering a Sense of the Sacred: Conversations with Thomas Berry.* Reading Thomas Berry's writings can be challenging. In her book, Toben makes Berry's often lofty language and abstract concepts understandable and personally accessible. Where Berry speaks of cosmology, Toben brings the small violet growing in the middle of the path into the conversation. She says the book is "a love story of learning to see through the eyes of the heart."

IN NATURE

March 2013 · Vol. 34, No. 1

Around me the trees stir in their leaves and call out "stay awhile."

—MARY OLIVER,
"When I Am Among the Trees"

Walking in the forest these February days and sitting by a creek swollen with recent rain, I notice a whiff of early spring in the air. As I listen for deep voices in the moving waters,

I hear the early music of the spring peepers, the sound of the wind in the trees, and the birdsongs, blending together to create a symphony of early spring. The awakening forest floor smells of acrid damp soil and decaying leaves. The mosses on the forest floor glow bright green and the buds on the trees appear to be swelling with growth. Tiny speckled foliage of the trout lily pushes up through the forest floor between the brown leaves. The early morning and late afternoon light lengthens as the sun begins its return, reminding me of an experience I had in February a few years ago when I went to the forest before dawn to spend the day in silence.

It was dark and cold when I arrived at 5:00 a.m., so I paced back and forth to keep warm. As the sky began to turn gold, I noticed the first rays of sunlight touch the base of a nearby tree and slowly move up the trunk and I began to weep with relief. The sun was returning and bringing warmth and light to creation. As the sun's energy warmed my cold body, my heart filled with gratitude for the miracle of that moment.

I go to the forest trails searching for those magical times when my soul reminds me that I am a part of creation. I long to relive those crucial moments when the earth wraps me in her arms and whispers that I belong to her. I am reminded over and over that we live in a beautiful universe. Experiencing ourselves as creatures belonging to the natural world can be transforming and numinous, leading us back to our sacred connection with the earth.

IN NATURE

June 2013

To be human is to become visible
while carrying what is hidden as a gift to others.
To remember the other world in this world
is to live in your true inheritance.
—DAVID WHYTE,
"What to Remember When Waking"

Spending time in nature feeds my spirit and soul. Walking in the forest, sitting quietly on a bench in a garden, lying in a hammock immersed in the green of spring trees, and digging in the earth, planting flowers and vegetables, all open me to a deep connection with the earth.

As a child, I knew I was a part of an enchanted world. I would often go into the forest for solace and companionship. I lost this connection for many years while I was busy growing a family and career. Now, in my elder years, I am being called home again to the natural world. These days I am recovering a rapport with the trees, birds, and creatures of the land. As I practice going beyond aesthetic appreciation, dropping below my senses into an intuitive knowing, I find the way to my soul. Many people experience this in meditation and other spiritual practices. I have joyfully rediscovered that my path is in the natural world. Because of this, I eagerly responded to Pat Webster's desire to create a workshop focused on nature.

RCWMS sponsored "Our Nature, In Nature" at Timberlake Earth Sanctuary April 19–21, where twelve women gathered for a weekend camping retreat. Pat designed the workshop, and I assisted. Pat's training as a vision quest guide and leader with the School of Lost Borders in California inspired her to create a local program grounded in the earth-based spirituality of the Medicine Wheel.

The weekend's teachings were focused on the wisdom of indigenous people who honor the sacredness of the natural world and understand the many ways the natural world mirrors our own nature. We gathered in circle, listened to the teachings of each compass direction and then carried questions for reflection as we wandered the trails, paying close attention to what was being mirrored to us. Afterward we sat in council sharing what had been revealed to us. Through our sharing we became a tribe of twelve. At the end of the workshop, a few of us said we would like to stay at Timberlake and live each day like this; in communion with the numinous in ourselves, the land and each other…in love with our life. Many of us yearn for ways to share this wisdom with our larger communities and with the children in our lives. We join with other companions to work on programs that focus on protecting our beloved planet earth and to connect us with the sacred in the natural world.

SECTION II

ELDER WOMEN'S SPIRITUALITY PROJECT

THE CREATION OF the Elder Women's Spirituality Project grew out of Anita's recognition that, just as menopause could be reclaimed as an opportunity for insight and empowerment, the years from the age of sixty until death could be recast as a time of deep spiritual growth and moral action. Conceived of as the Elder Women's Network and known informally as The Elder Women Project, Anita collaborated with others to offer experiential programs that empower women to claim the wisdom of their lived experiences, to live with authenticity growing toward wholeness, and to leave a lasting legacy for future generations.

In this section, you will find some of the founding documents for the Elder Women's Spirituality Project, followed by material about its work over the years.

ORIGINS

On July 15, 2010, fourteen neighborhood women gathered at my house to view the film *For the Next 7 Generations*. Most of them had never heard of the Thirteen Grandmothers and were visibly and deeply moved. An eighty-two-year-old grandmother from Honduras was visiting her daughter and attended despite the fact that she did not speak English.

Her young granddaughter, about twenty years old, came and translated for her during the film. The women ranged in age from eighteen to eighty-two. When the showing was over, I asked them what touched them, what surprised them, and what images or thoughts they were leaving with. One particular woman, with tears in her eyes, said that she felt so connected to all the women in the room because, like the grandmothers, we were also a very diverse group sharing in a circle of women. Another woman said she was touched that the grandmothers from all over the world came together and grew to love each other and were so accepting of each other's traditions.

ELDER WOMEN'S NETWORK: A PROSPECTUS

When the grandmothers speak, the earth will heal.
—ATTRIBUTED AS HOPI PROPHECY

More women are entering their sixties, seventies, and eighties with better health, higher levels of education, greater work experience, and more resources than ever before. We have choices our mothers and grandmothers never dreamed of, and we can now ask, "How do I want to live the rest of my 'one wild and precious life?'"[3] Each of us was born with a gift for the world, and as we grow older, the desire to share that gift grows more urgent.

We have lived with meaning and purpose and want meaningful action to continue to be central in our lives. But we do not want to go to more meetings or form new organizations. We want to shepherd our energy and focus our action on what is most important. We want to join together in community and lend our voices and actions to what we love and value.

Many elder women are expressing deep concern for future generations and deep dismay over the declining health of our earth. Women who were inspired and changed by the feminist movement are leading the way, and many are looking to the indigenous women of the world for wisdom and guidance. The archetype of the powerful wise old woman, that has been all too absent from the western world, is now rising in the land.

My goal is to inspire elder women to be a force for peace and justice, especially in North Carolina. I envision elder women coming together in local community groups connected to each other through the Resource Center for Women and Ministry in the South (RCWMS). Many elder women are already contributing to local community organizations. An Elder Women's Network would encourage and support them further by linking them with other women doing similar work. An Elder Women's network proposes a visionary possibility that circles of wise grandmothers can help to transform our society into a more peaceful and compassionate home. Elder women can inspire one another to give their voices, wisdom, and presence in support of the sacredness of life. My hope is that women will find community and support for their spiritual journeys as they work on behalf of their deepest concerns.

There are many things that groups of elder women might do. One group could share their love of the natural world with groups of young people, teach children about gardening, or join forces with a local environmental organization. Another group might choose to express their views on a public issue. Another group of wise women elders could change a quarrelsome encounter in a public hearing to a more cooperative process just by their strong presence.

The Network will:

- Offer inspirational and experience-based programs led by local elder women.
- Offer workshops to train facilitators for circles and councils.
- Show the film *For the Next 7 Generations* to various groups.
- Convene councils afterward, and teach the council process.
- Encourage participants to identify an issue of concern.
- Support them in gathering a local circle.
- Gather and maintain a database of participants.
- RCWMS (www.rcwms.org) will serve as a central clearinghouse, offering information, inspiration, contacts, resources, and website links.

THE FILM

The International Council of Thirteen Indigenous Grand-mothers is an inspirational force of love and wisdom guiding us to new paths of service in our families and communi-ties. Their film, *For the Next 7 Generations*, shows how elder women can come together and work for balance and wisdom in the world.

The Thirteen Grandmothers are respected medicine women and shamans from the Americas, the Arctic Circle, Asia, and Africa. Each woman received a message, in vision or prophecy, that at a crucial moment she would be called onto the world stage to help lead the human race into a new era of healing, cooperation, and peace. In 2004, they came together in upstate New York, formed the council, and set to work. The Grandmothers' agenda is simple, yet poten-tially revolutionary: "Our No. 1 priority is promoting peace and good relationships with everyone in the world," says Grandmother Mona Polacca, an Arizona Hopi/Havasupai/Tewa. The film's award-winning director, Carole Hart, says, "They are helping people see the world from an indigenous perspective, which says that we are connected by the web of life, not just people but every living thing on the planet." They model their message by visiting each other's home-lands, praying and creating ceremony together. Adds film-maker Hart, "This film will awaken those who are asleep at the wheel, and inspire the rapidly growing numbers of peo-ple who are working to create peace, justice, harmony, and balance across the planet. With the ways the Grandmothers show us, we can sustain our planet so that our planet can sustain us."

My hope is that elder women will see the film, join in council process afterward and be inspired to create a circle or council in their community around a common concern. The support of other like-minded women can empower these groups to take action on behalf of what they love.

ELDER WOMEN NEWS

August 2012

Aging today has become an improvisational art form calling for imagination and willingness to learn.

—MARY CATHERINE BATESON,
  Composing a Future Life

More women are entering their sixties, seventies, and eighties with better health, higher levels of education, greater work experience, and more resources than ever before. We have time and choices our mothers and grandmothers never dreamed of, and we can now ask, with poet Mary Oliver, how do I want to live the rest of my "one wild and precious life?"[4] Each of us was born with a gift to give to the world, and as we grow older, we have an opportunity to "give back."

In May of 2012, RCWMS received a $20,000 grant from the Kalliopeia Foundation in support of our Elder Women's Spirituality Project. Funds will be used over the course of the year to expand elder women's spiritual and creative development and support their ongoing engagement in the world. Programs will include workshops on spirituality, writing, creativity, vital aging, legacy, and end-of-life issues, as well as a film series.

ELDER WOMEN NEWS

September 2012

Mother Earth is a conscious, alive, and responsive being—a goddess in Her own right.

—THIRTEEN INDIGENOUS GRANDMOTHERS,
   For the Next 7 Generations

Growing up in the middle of the last century, we had much more freedom to explore the natural world than children do today. Many weekends, after-school time, and summer months were spent playing outside in parks, woodlands, streams, and fields. I remember the delight of creating playhouses in the rhododendron bushes and long evenings of hide and seek in the sparkling dusk of summer evenings. Many of us were comforted by "special places" outside to which we retreated for reflection and respite. Frogs, butterflies, and clouds stimulated our imagination. We had a tangible experience of belonging to the natural world.

Many of us now wonder how to share our spiritual knowing with the busy overscheduled children in our lives.

We ask ourselves what kind of legacy do we want to leave our grandchildren? What stories can we tell children to awaken their sense of wonder and oneness with the earth? What love stories for the earth do we have to share with them?

ELDER WOMEN NEWS

October 2012

What did the tree learn from the earth to be able to talk with the sky?

—PABLO NERUDA, *The Book of Questions*

This past week in a women's circle, we each played with scissors, colored papers and markers creating an image of a tree that was an expression of ourselves. When we were finished, we placed our images on the table and noticed how different they were and how they reflected the essence of each of us.

Later at home, I placed my image on my desk and continue to be awed by how my tree image is teaching me about my spirituality. She invites me to explore deeply into my roots, she shows me I am "ensouled" in her, and she reminds me that out of my brokenness and wrinkles, new blooming is happening.

Exploring our creativity through movement, simple art projects, free writing, and music calls our attention to the wisdom of our senses and opens our hearts. We learn about what we know in our bodies and in our souls.

ELDER WOMEN NEWS

~~~~~~~~~~~~~~~~~~~~~~~~~~~~~~

November 2012

What did the tree learn from the earth to be able to talk with the sky?

—PABLO NERUDA, *The Book of Questions*

In these colorful days of autumn our attention is drawn to how rapidly and magnificently the colors in the trees are changing and how fast the leaves are falling. We can sense and smell the change of seasons in the air. It is not yet winter, but the north wind reminds us how near the cold season is.

Make sure to take a quiet contemplative walk among the autumn trees, listening and noticing closely what is happening. Take time to reflect on your connection to the trees, the wind, the busy birds, and the squirrels. What resonates within you? Maybe you will notice a welling up of wonder and gratitude for the beauty and creative unfolding of life around you. Maybe you will sense an intimate connection between you and a particular tree. Maybe your heart will be moved to sing or write a praise-song for the earth. May your soul recognize the sacred in the natural world.

ELDER WOMEN NEWS

December 2012

To be able to notice the less obvious beauty, to appreciate it, to change perspective for a time is a type of quiet, a way of rest. . . . Attending to small things in front of us becomes a way of self-renewal and self-refreshment.

—SHARON SALZBERG, *Lovingkindness: The Revolutionary Art of Happiness*

On the first day of December, Barbara Anderson and I led a program for RCWMS entitled "A Quiet Day." The workshop grew out of our observation of the wisdom of the natural world. In December, after the abundance of the autumn harvest, nature enters a time of deep rest and quiet. The leaves have fallen, the tree sap has drawn itself down and deep, and many creatures are in hibernation. We humans are a part of the natural world. Our bodies and souls yearn to join our kin in rest and solitude. At the same time, our culture pulls us out to shop, consume and party. So we designed the workshop to reflect this split and offer practices to renew, restore and rejuvenate ourselves moment by moment during the upcoming weeks rather than recover afterward. One of the practices was a walking meditation outdoors, paying full attention to our surroundings, offering silent loving kindness blessings to ourselves and to others we encountered on our walk, such as a dog, a person working in their yard, a tiny flower growing near a gate, and the trees. Carrying peace and love for ourselves and for others and all beings creates a felt sense of blessing and gratitude, an aura of ease and contentment. We are alive and new in the present moment.

LOOKING BACK ON THE FIRST YEAR OF THE ELDER WOMEN'S SPIRITUALITY PROJECT

Late 2012

What a year this has been for the Elder Women's Spirituality Project! The grant from the Kalliopeia Foundation for $20,000 in May jump-started our programs and gave enormous energy to our efforts. Now, approaching the end of 2012, I want to reflect on what we have created.

We started in early September with the workshop "Harvesting Our Stories, Collecting Our Wisdom," led by Liz Dowling-Sender and myself. One participant said, "The only thing we own is our stories," and another woman said, "We are all like peaches, ripe and a bit bruised by life." The day was filled with writing prompts, reading to each other and being deeply moved by being a part of the same generation of women. A group agreed to meet once a month for the rest of 2012 and continue the harvesting process.

On the autumn equinox in September we offered a workshop at Timberlake Earth Sanctuary entitled, "When the Grandmothers Speak, the Earth Will Heal," led by Carolyn Toben and myself. As we shared stories of our childhood sense of wonder and connection with the natural world, we touched into our natural radiance and the power of imagination. Many women noted how the deep bedrock of our souls resonates with the land and each other as we slow to a different pace. We know that today's children do not have these experiences. We committed to sharing something of what we learned with the children and young people in our lives.

We want to help elder women claim their wisdom and their voice, to lead with their hearts and to repair our sacred connection with the earth.

Longing for women's sacred community…sitting in circle with candle at center, an altar of our own making.

The title of our program might evoke a smile because "embracing elderhood" implies an optimistic outlook on a life stage characterized in part by harsh realities. Be assured that this program does indeed embrace an optimistic approach to aging, but it also provides a safe setting to voice the grief, anger, and challenges associated with the final quadrant of life. By feeling and sharing the troubling elements of aging, we are more enabled to discover the joyful opportunities of the elder years.

The Chinese word for crisis is composed of two separate characters—one for danger and one for opportunity. Entering the final quadrant of life is like this: a dangerous opportunity (like all the major life transitions). As we approach the threshold of elderhood, extraordinary challenges and choices await us.

Opportunities include:

- to seek the deepest meaning of our elder years
- to release our old stories and experience the glorious freedom of elderhood
- to remember the gifts of who we have become through our lifetime of working, seeking, and learning
- to awaken to our most potent dreams and discover renewed purpose
- to learn new paths of service to our families and communities, giving back in gratitude and joy so that the next generations will be nurtured by our love and mentored by our wisdom

Dangers are there as well:

- increased chance of illness or declining physical and mental health
- distress as we discover that travel, material comforts, and leisure after so many years of labor and striving do not fulfill our longing for meaning and purpose
- desires to remain competitive in the marketplace as that phase of our life comes to a close
- attempts to remain forever young
- withdrawal from society, as self-protection from a world full of radical change, disruption, and conflict
- attachment to old traumas, grievances and unfinished business, allowing them to define and restrict our lives

Perhaps you feel you're approaching the season when your habitual activities are coming to a close. You might have a heightened awareness of changes in your body and of physical limitations. These changes might evoke sadness—or fear that there's nothing to take the place of your former way of life or nothing to fill your days with meaning. And yet, you find yourself longing to serve your community in ever greater ways.

"Embracing Elderhood: A Soulcraft Exploration" offers the chance to be together in sacred communion with others facing these challenges and dangerous opportunities. We'll explore emotions and difficulties related to aging. We'll engage in nature-based tasks on the land that open us to the extraordinary fulfillment available in elderhood. And we'll share our stories. In these perilous and challenging times, the mature voices and strong presences of true elders are essential to the survival and vitality of our human and more-than-human communities.

ELDER WOMEN NEWS

January 2013
To be blessed in life, one must learn to die
To be blessed in death, one must learn to live.
—PHILIPPE DUPLESSIS-MORNAY, *Mémoires Et Correspondance*

Last January more than twenty courageous women participated in a new RCWMS venture called the "End of Life

Series." We met in a cozy living room that provided a supportive container in which to contemplate the taboo topic of death. Many women commented that they had never discussed death so openly or personally.

The series was so well received that we decided to offer it again this year. The purpose of the series is to prepare as consciously and compassionately as we can for the end of our lives.

We will consider many questions:

- What experiences have we had with death and what have we learned from them?
- What are the essential conversations we need to have with our loved ones and professional support team to ensure our wishes are carried out?
- What are our wishes?
- What are our choices?
- What documents do we need and what is the legacy we want to leave our family and community?

Contemplating these questions and discovering our answers can bring a sense of deep peace to our lives, as we are no longer running from the fear of death. We can then cherish the precious time remaining to us by wholeheartedly embracing the future that beckons us.

ELDER WOMEN NEWS

April 2013

Mother's Day as we celebrate it today has its origins in women's work for peace. In 1872 Julia Ward Howe proposed that June 2 be established as a "Mother's Day for Peace." Howe was devoted to both pacifism and women's suffrage and envisioned Mother's Day as a time for mothers to join together and work for peace.

In a spirit of gratitude for women's ongoing work for peace, and in honor of Mother's Day, the Elder Women's Project would like to invite you to recognize a special woman in your life by supporting and strengthening RCWMS with a donation of cash or stock. We will send a personalized card to the honoree, if living, or a card to the family of your loved one if you provide honoree's name and address.

ELDER WOMEN NEWS

June 2013

To be human is to become visible
while carrying what is hidden as a gift to others.
To remember the other world in this world
is to live in your true inheritance.
—DAVID WHYTE, "What to Remember When Waking"

Spending time in the world of nature feeds my spirit and my soul. Walking in the forest, sitting quietly on a bench in a garden, lying in a hammock immersed in the green of spring trees, and digging in the earth all open me to a deep connection with the earth.

As a child, I knew I was a part of an enchanted world. I would often go into the forest for solace and companionship. This connection was lost for many years while I was busy growing a family and career. Now, in my elder years, I am being called home again to the natural world. These days I am recovering a rapport with the trees, birds, and creatures of the land. As I practice going beyond aesthetic appreciation, dropping below my senses into an intuitive knowing, I find the way to my soul. I have rediscovered that my spiritual path is in the natural world.

ELDER WOMEN NEWS

August 2013

If stories come to you, care for them. And learn to give them away where they are needed. Sometimes a person needs a story more than food to stay alive.

—BARRY LOPEZ, *Crow and Weasel*

I have been enjoying a respite from the busyness of the school year and reveling in the rest and quiet of a lush green summertime. In these calm moments, I have dreamt of new programs for the fall and winter to come.

I am very excited about a workshop that Lyndall Hare and I will be offering on September 7 in Durham, NC called "The Art of Aging: Celebrating Elderhood." This workshop will invite us to share our experience of aging, and will help us to move from a model of aging based in decline and diminishment to one grounded in deepening and growth. We will explore the meaning of conscious elderhood and consider the tasks involved in becoming an elder. Using ritual, storytelling and contemplative practices, this experiential event is designed to awaken us to the adventure of conscious aging and enable us to harvest the many gifts of enlivenment.

ELDER WOMEN NEWS

September 2013

Aging is not 'lost youth' but a new stage of opportunity and strength.

—BETTY FRIEDAN, *"How to Live Longer, Better, Wiser"*

Twenty-two women attended "The Art of Aging" workshop on a beautiful early fall day in Durham. The intention of the workshop was to give participants a taste of the inner work of eldering, covering such topics as life review, deepening our spiritual connection, and creating legacy. It is my hope that an ongoing group will meet regularly to continue exploring the opportunities and gifts to be discovered in our expanded years of life. Many of us hunger to be together sharing our life stories and contemplative practices.

ELDER WOMEN NEWS

October 2013

For the unlearned, old age is winter; for the learned it is the season of the harvest.

—ATTRIBUTED TO THE TALMUD

May you be given a wisdom with the eye of your soul to see this beautiful time of harvesting.

—JOHN O'DONOHUE, *To Bless the Space Between Us*

Have you seen the bountiful harvest of fall vegetables at the farmers' markets? The abundance of deep colors and rich nutrients in the vegetables reminds me of the rich, deep bounty we can harvest from our lives. As we unearth and gather up our life stories, and reflect on our experiences, we harvest wisdom to share with others. Harvesting is a vital task of eldering. One way to do this is through journaling practices that enable us to till the soil of our inner experience and bring forth treasured stories.

ELDER WOMEN NEWS

January 2014

By whatever means, hold close to what you love and make it a life work
to love more and more of this precious world.

—FRANCIS WELLER, *"Reclaiming Our Indigenous Soul"*

I stood in my driveway with a friend looking at the January full moon shining through the bony branches of the bare trees above my house. The silver moon creates a beacon in the black night sky, illuminating a path between us. What is it that stirs in my chest as I stand on the earth and look at the winter moon and her companion, Jupiter? It is my heart calling me to wonder in awe at the magnificence of our ever-expanding universe. It is my soul filling with gratitude for our precious earth and sky. I am called to reflection, to ponder what it is the moon is mirroring to me. She mirrors the sacred universe.

ELDER WOMEN NEWS

February 2014

For those who embrace the gifts reserved for age . . . old age becomes freedom, becomes the dance.

—BARBARA A. MOWAT, "Introduction" to Helen Luke's *Old Age*

I just finished reading a deeply meaningful book entitled *Ripening Time: Inside Stories for Aging with Grace*, by author Sherry Ruth Anderson. Using the art of inner inquiry while challenging our culture's lies about aging, the author illuminates the challenges and gifts possible in our elder years. The issue is not to look for a map or try to know the map, the issue is to be the map. This book gives us a compass for the journey. With humor, wisdom and compassion, she offers stories of elders harvesting the bounty of their years. If you are curious about the blessings, losses, hopes and truths of growing old, you will want to read this empowering book and share it with others.

ELDER WOMEN NEWS

March 2014

Someone once told me that all wisdom could be found in the natural world.

During the winter months, I have practiced taking my direction from the natural world. My intention has been to be still, to rest, to go slow, and to deepen like the roots of a tree reaching for underground water. Trees are not dormant in the winter; the roots grow deeper into the earth searching for nutrients. I have been gathering nourishment from resting and slowing. While this is not my natural state, I have found this practice both challenging and nurturing. Now that spring is awakening, I feel my energy rising, and my task is to integrate what I have learned and be mindful of my choices.

ELDER WOMEN NEWS

April 2014

One could say that the whole of life lies in seeing.
—PIERRE TEILHARD DE CHARDIN, *The Human Phenomenon*

Twenty-three women gathered on Tuesday, April 8, 2014, for a retreat at Timberlake Earth Sanctuary entitled "When the Grandmothers Speak, the Earth will Heal." The title is based on a wisdom saying from the Hopi in the Southwest. It is my understanding that the essence of grandmother energy is unconditional love and respect for the children and families of all living beings. Women do not need to have birthed children to carry grandmother energy. All who cherish the earth and her creatures embody grandmother energy.

The intention of the retreat was to offer experiences to reconnect the participants with the wonder, awe, and the sacred in the natural world that we knew as children, so we might share our knowing with the children in our lives to help repair our sacred relationship with the earth. We shared stories in small groups, went on a guided earth walk to learn skills of awakening our senses, had a solo time of reflection on the land and returned to share in circle our discoveries. It was a blessed day. We unplugged from the technology of our daily lives and plugged into the blessed land.

ELDER WOMEN NEWS

May 2014

There are a thousand ways to kneel and kiss the ground.
—ATTRIBUTED TO RUMI

Have you walked the lush forest trails or visited the local gardens lately? If you have, I know you are aware of the rich green abundance of our spring. Every tree and flowering plant is well nourished with rain and sunlight. The butterflies, hummingbirds, and frogs have returned to our land. The songbirds begin their morning symphony early in the day before sunrise and continue all day long. Spring in North Carolina this year is particularly inviting as the temperatures are milder, the cool breezes enticing us to come outdoors to look, listen and feel the beauty of our earth home. As nature awakens, we are called to wake up to the mystery and wildness within the natural world and within ourselves. Give yourself the gift of a contemplative immersion in nature, out of which may come a prayer of gratitude and blessing for our beloved earth.

ELDER WOMEN NEWS

June 2014

The Art of Conscious Aging monthly meetings are growing a special community. A core group shows up every month, and there are newcomers at every gathering. We begin our circle by lighting a central candle with the intention of creating sacred space. Each woman then says her name and how many years of lived experience she brings to the circle. Our ages usually range from fifty to eighty-six. Leadership is provided by the participants and the format includes introduction of the topic by the leader, some personal reflection time, small group sharing, and then large group sharing.

Our topics over the past eight months have been varied but are focused on the experiences of aging and the difference between being old and becoming an elder. In May, we spoke about myths, lies, and truths about aging, challenging the cultural norms of aging as a process only of decay and despair. In June, we explored some of the tasks of elderhood, such as telling our life stories, sharing our challenges, and the call to deepen our spiritual life. Many of us have found our circle to be a deeply meaningful experience filled with humor, empathic connection, and a sense of kinship.

ELDER WOMEN NEWS

August 2014

We forget that the water cycle and the life cycle are one.
—ATTRIBUTED TO JACQUES COUSTEAU

Grandmothers and elders are gathering around the world to offer blessings and prayers for the healing of our waters. We act as stewards of the future, as coming generations will not be able to survive without clean water. We cannot create water. Water is a sacred mystery.

The media is filled with news that our lakes, streams, and rivers are contaminated with heavy metals and toxins due to industrial pollution. When government and industry rush to begin "fracking," we come to say, "Wake up; pay attention!" The water must be considered. We have reached a critical juncture. Either we continue to contaminate our precious water with toxins and carcinogens or we wake up and say, "Enough! We value clean water over gas."

Water is sacred. Life is unsustainable without clean water. We want to come together in prayer for the healing and protection of our waters.

We invite all concerned people of all faiths to join us in thanking and blessing the water. Here are a few ways you can bless the water:

- Simply fill a small container with water to represent all the waters on planet earth. Hold this water in meditation to infuse it with love and positive intentions. When you can, pour some of this charged water into a natural body of water.

- Gather friends and go to a local body of water. Pray for the water and apologize to the water for pollution and disrespect. You can offer prayers of love, gratitude, and respect to the water by holding both of your hands out to the water. Then offer energy from your heart to the water through your hands. Use your own words of appreciation intending that the prayers will flow to all the waters of the earth.

ELDER WOMEN NEWS

October 2014

We are not human beings on a spiritual journey, we are spiritual beings on a human journey.

—Variously attributed to Pierre Teilhard de Chardin and George Gurdjiieff

As the cool breezes and shorter days announce the arrival of early autumn, I pause to reflect on the abundance the Elder Women Project is manifesting. The Art of Conscious Aging group has gathered monthly for a year, supporting women as they contemplate what it means to grow into elderhood. As they consider the opportunities and gifts of waking up to their life now, many feel empowered to move beyond the cultural definitions of aging into the challenge of conscious eldering. A conscious elder feels the need to attend to their inner soul and spiritual development through reflection and contemplation and to find a way to express their wholeness in service to the community.

In October, an intergenerational retreat called "Herons Walk on Water's Edge" will take place. Young women and elder women will come together in sacred circle to bring forth our authentic selves. "Heron's Walk" will offer contemplative, mindful, and ceremonial practices in the natural world. The retreat invites participants to return to a natural sacred pace where we are closest to the Deep Mystery in service to the healing of ourselves, each other, and the earth.

ELDER WOMEN NEWS— GRATITUDE

December 2014

Gratitude makes sense of our past, brings peace for today, and creates a vision for tomorrow.

—MELODY BEATTIE, *The Language of Letting Go*

In October, a group of eleven women ages twenty-seven to seventy-four gathered for four days at a rural retreat center to explore through imagination, intuition, sensing, and embodied knowing, their relationship with themselves, each other, and the natural world. All were encouraged to leave their cell phones, watches and computers at home so they might be more receptive to the messages present for them in nature. Ritual and ceremony led the women deeper into their own experience and solo time on the land supported them in listening to their hearts.

Each day, the women came together in council to speak from their hearts and to listen with the ears of their hearts. Their transformation was apparent over the four days as faces became softer and more radiant, tears and laughter emerged more gently, and dancing and drumming intensified. The women uncovered their authentic voices and found their innate courage as they deepened their experience of the sacred in the natural world.

In this season of thankfulness, I offer deep gratitude to Sherylyn Pitt, who designed and led the "Herons Walk" retreat, and to all the participants who fearlessly showed up and participated with great heart. The power of an intergenerational women's retreat impacted all of us and we hope to offer this again in the future. I am also grateful to the Kalliopeia Foundation, whose grant support funds scholarships, and to RCWMS for all their support.

ELDER WOMEN NEWS

April 2015

Abide at the center of your being for the more you leave it the less you learn.

—ATTRIBUTED TO LAO TZU

As more of us live longer, we are discovering a new stage of life beyond childhood, adulthood, and middle age that is more than just old age. As those of us over sixty contemplate how we want to live into our future years, we have choices to make. How do we answer vital questions such as "Who am I now? What gives my life meaning at this time? How do I want to live the years remaining to me? What is the gift that has been placed inside of me that is mine to bring to my people?"

A movement is growing in our country called "conscious eldering" or conscious aging. This movement challenges us to practice being conscious, awake, and intentional in our elder years. It challenges us to realize that getting older can be a rich and rewarding spiritual adventure rather than simply a time of deterioration or amusing ourselves until we die. We have a fresh opportunity to grow, learn, and serve through practices that deepen our wisdom and presence. One practice that can help us claim our elderhood and wisdom is "life review," which includes exploring who we have been, who we are now, the gifts we have to bring forward, and the life lessons we have to share.

ELDER WOMEN NEWS

September 2015

The core of our work is to restore soul to the earth and to ourselves.

—ATTRIBUTED TO CHELLIS GLENDINNING

As the last days of summer slowly get shorter and the sun moves toward the fall equinox, my body and soul anticipate being out of doors in the freshness of early autumn. My heart leaps with anticipation as the temperature cools and the crisp clear air calls me back to the forest. During long luscious hours sitting quietly among the trees in the forest I remember my "creatureness" and all the ways I belong to the earth and to life.

This fall I am especially looking forward to "Herons Walk," a retreat in early October led by Sherylyn Pitt and myself. We co-led this retreat in 2014. Here are two participant quotes from last year:

"Experiencing Heron's Walk was a doorway to meet the real me. I was guided to find out what is most important and how to speak from the heart. With these new practices, it has allowed me to become the most authentic I believe I have ever been."

"This was a pilgrimage of my heart and soul. This was no ordinary spiritual community. This was a gathering of women from all ages and walks of life, joining together to explore sacred mystery. This was a journey of a lifetime. I returned home from Heron's Walk a changed woman; a woman with a renewed curiosity for the divine in all of us."

Immersion in sacred circle and solo time in the natural world are deeply healing practices for our feminine spirit.

ELDER WOMEN NEWS

March 2016

We are living in a world that is absolutely transparent and the divine is shining through it all the time.

—THOMAS MERTON

The exquisite trout lilies are blooming in the forest. The creeks and streams are full of singing waters. The early flowering trees and plants are showcasing themselves around town. My body and heart respond with ambivalence as I am called to loosen my attachment to the deep quiet contemplation of wintertime and gently move into the active energetic renewal of spring.

In the past, I often lurched into hyperactivity in response to spring and quickly found myself exhausted and overcommitted. I have learned in recent years to give clear attention to this change and move as consciously as I can. Going for walks in the forest during February, March, and April eases my transition. I invite you to go to the wooded paths and walk before the trees become leafed out. Notice the shadows of the trees on the forest floor and how far you can see. What early harbingers of spring do you see and hear? How does the divine speak to you through what you behold?

ELDER WOMEN NEWS

July 2016

Walking in the forest with a dear friend on Saturday, we marveled at the deep blue of the sky, the lush green of the trees, and the stunning diversity of the plants along the path. A bubbling creek shimmered in the bright sunlight and birdsong filled the air. We both felt wrapped in profound beauty and divine creativity.

All this beauty seemed a stark contrast to the cruelty in our world and the violent and destructive political events in our state and country.

When I walk through the woods, I am nourished by the richness of the life around me. When we put ourselves in the natural world, we have a chance to breathe in spiritual nourishment. I leave the woods refreshed and full of gratitude. Being in nature can renew us and help us sustain our efforts to serve our communities.

Savoring and serving, being and doing, receiving and giving—these are the critical concerns of elders wanting to act consciously in the world. And these require balance and practice. What practices uplift and guide you?

ELDER WOMEN NEWS—THE GREAT TURNING

December 2016

[This piece was written by Jeanette Stokes.]

Anita McLeod is at home recovering from surgery. She was greatly moved by a recent daily meditation from Fr. Richard Rohr, Franciscan founder of the Center for Action and Contemplation, and asked that we share some of his thoughts with you. You can read his full post by clicking the link below.

Rohr, along with fellow thinkers Joanna Macy, David Korten (author of *The Great Turning*), and Bill Plotkin, calls for humanity to transition from what Macy calls "the Industrial Growth Society to a Life-Sustaining Society."[5] They urge us to confront the destructive effects of climate change.

Anita believes that this is the time of the Great Turning. That's what this frightening presidential election was about. The Divine Feminine is with us as lover and warrior. She is calling elder women to stand up for the precious earth and water and creatures. For ourselves. For our children.

She recommends that you go for a gratitude walk in the forest or around your neighborhood. You can go by yourself or with a friend. Thank all the growing things you see: the grasses, the mosses, the mushrooms, the creatures, and the earth. Thank anything that delights you. Smile at people you meet along the way, even people you don't know. Spread love.

SECTION III

OTHER WRITINGS

OVER THE YEARS, Anita was a keen participant in and observer of her world. Many writings in this section were not dated, so they are organized by themes such as the stages of women's physical, emotional and spiritual development. Included in this theme are an article she wrote for publication in *Conscious Living, Conscious Aging* and selections from *Turning Points*, an intergenerational writing workshop and publication led by Anita and Rebecca Welper that epitomize Anita's ability to weave in and lift up other voices. Other themes are conscious aging, her deep connection to the natural world, the loss of friends, and her wise appreciation for life's nuances in the homily she wrote for a young couple.

PUBERTY AND MENOPAUSE

I have come to know that as puberty is the gateway to adulthood, menopause is the passageway to elderhood. They are both experiences of transformation, of body, mind and spirit. At some point in a young girl's life usually around the age of eleven or twelve, when she is full of energy and intelligence, when she knows herself and what she wants, a major physical event occurs. Due to some great mystery, a cascade of hormones and neurotransmitters begins and she enters a change of life. Her physical body, emotional self, mind and spirit are profoundly altered. Strange urges well up from inside of her. Her focus now is on others, rather than herself. She yearns to be accepted by others and loses touch with her inner guidance. Her locus of control is outside herself.

Then somewhere between forty-five and fifty, a woman enters another major life transition that has the potential to change her mind, body and spirit in profound ways if she heeds the messages of her inner guidance. Responding to the changes rather than fighting them reveals the gifts of menopause. One of the gifts of paying attention is you have an opportunity to reconnect with the wise young playful girl you were before puberty. As Maxine Kumin said, "When Sleeping Beauty wakes up/ she is almost fifty years old."[6]

AFTER MENOPAUSE

Menopause is over. I am now in the postmenopausal years. I am sixty-three years of age and I am asking myself, "What now?" The question is, paraphrasing the poet Mary Oliver, "What do I want to do with the rest of my one wild and precious life?"[7]

I want to have conversations with women over sixty about their valued experiences, their dreams for themselves, their passions for the future and their soul yearnings. I want to have conversations of depth and searching with women of all ages. I want to deepen my experience, open my mind to fresh ideas and be touched in my heart and soul by the experience of living. I want to focus on what is possible and what is true. For that, I need solitude to know what it is I know and to expand my awareness. So, sitting in silence first thing each morning, and also journaling each morning. Lighting a candle, surrounded by the four elements of earth, air, fire and water, to begin and end my sacred time.

My desires feel like they are few. Time with myself, time with family, loved ones and women friends, time outdoors, creative time writing and sewing, learning and teaching, and going on pilgrimages to places that inspire and quicken the divinity within me. Finding the balance of filling with energy and expressing (expending) energy...the feminine receptivity and the masculine taking action. There must be play and laughter!

TURNING SIXTY

January 18, 2004

I am devouring Faulkner Fox's book, *Dispatches from a Not-So-Perfect Life* and thinking what is it I can say about being sixty in my own voice that might resonate with others. I connect with her rawness, honesty, and truth-telling, as well as her humor. I am moved by the clarity of her voice. She started writing about her own experiences and feelings and then began interviewing women and asking questions. My questions could be...What has changed since you turned sixty? What draws most of your time and attention these days? What do you love most?

When I turned sixty, I decided I wanted to have a quiet intimate celebration at my home with four close women friends and that I wanted to cook for them. I do not remember what I prepared—maybe spinach quiche and salad—I do remember that I used my mother's china. She had been given her china by her coworkers at Bell Labs in New York City where she worked before she was married. I remember washing and hand drying the china as a young girl on holiday occasions following strict admonitions to handle each piece very carefully. On my sixtieth birthday, I honored my mother, Catherine Landsverk Swensen, with a toast, and found myself sensing her presence at my birthday party. I spoke of her gifts to me, her courage in breaking the cycle of violence in our family by choosing a kind, good man to marry and father their children.

I was struck that turning sixty was so different than turning fifty. When I became fifty years of age, I felt robust, energetic, hot, and very vital. I wanted to celebrate with many parties and gatherings in a Big Way. I wanted lots of people from all areas of my life, music and dancing, balloons, food and drink, the works. Very extrovert!

Turning sixty felt very personal and private. I did not want to celebrate with crowds and noise. I wanted a small intimate gathering of close women friends where we could have conversations of depth and meaning.

ENTERING OUR SIXTIES

May and June 2004

Entering our sixties can feel like walking into a strange new land. We have crossed the menopausal threshold and are no longer middle-aged women. We enter our elder years and our lives are not like our mother's and grandmother's lives. We talk about freedom. Freedom from roles as mother, daughter, wife, and workers. We discover we do not have many foremothers or guides for this time of life and realize the ancient wisdom of elder wise women down through history has been lost.

Living in a misogynist culture where the powerful feminine is greatly feared, few women think old age and power are compatible. We need new kinds of consciousness-raising for our elder years. This time to challenge the cultural devaluing of older women. We can help each other name the possibilities we hardly recognize or dare to put a name to. As Maxine Kumin suggests, we need each other as aging women to help us affirm and express our radical and radiant inner self that seems to carry the mystery and meaning of our life. At this time in history, there are over forty-five-million women entering their sixties. Our lives and attitudes were shaped by the women's movement. As Jean Shinoda Bolen observes, never before in recorded history have there been so many women with so much competence, experience, voice, independence and resources. The question is, what are we going to do with our expertise and resources.

It is time to challenge the negative stereotypes of older women and bring forth the wise woman within each of us in order to save our beloved Earth. The Native Americans say, "When the grandmothers speak, the earth will heal." In our search for wisdom and authenticity, we must develop practices to turn inward and listen to the voice of our inner wise woman to discover what we have learned from living, give voice to these truths and share them in community.

It is in this spirit that I offer gatherings for Women Over Sixty with the intention of creating a safe container where we can speak of our experience, be witnessed and nourished by others, and come to know and speak our wisdom in the world. We begin by asking how being sixty has affected us physically, emotionally, and spiritually. Many of us speak of the sense of vulnerability of our physical bodies. We are beginning to understand that our lives hang by a thread as we see friends develop illnesses and die. We experience various aches and pains. We do not have the endurance and resilience of our younger years. Some women report difficulty sleeping and lower energy levels. We know that our health, vitality and independence depend on regular exercise, healthy nutrition and rest. Emotionally, many women report feeling both more vulnerable and stronger than ever. As we recognize that everything is changing and we do not know what is coming down the road, we feel anxious. Yet we are more grounded and stable as we feel the emotional impact of our experiences. Relationships are more important and vital than ever. Several women have said the main focus of their life now is their spiritual journey. Recognizing the preciousness of this embodied life, many say they try to practice living in the present moment.

One major theme many women identified is the tension between a need for solitude and a need for community. Many women have been lifelong activists in their churches, neighborhoods, and in the public arena. Wanting more time for reflection and creativity while remaining aware of the overwhelming needs of the local and world community is a spoken tension and challenge. Creative urges to paint, garden, write, sculpt, sing, and pray can often conflict with our scheduled plans for the day. Creating sanctuary for ourselves is a strong desire for most of us.

FEAR

As I chose to go on a Vision Quest at the age of sixty-five, I was looking for a framework for the last third of my life. I signed up for Conscious Elder Vision Quest after reading a story of a woman who went into her fasting solo time searching for her "wildness." I found myself sobbing deeply as I read her story, recognizing a longing I had for my own inner wildness. I had little understanding what all this meant, but did recognize it as a call from my inner life that needed attention.

Fear was a central thread of the Vision Quest experience for me. I was so anxious at the beginning that I knocked the sunglasses off the head of one of the guides in my exuberance and nervousness to make a good impression. I made an impression alright!

Fear showed up for our entire Vision Quest group as we stood outside the sweat lodge preparing to enter and pray. We each stood separately wrapped in large bath towels in the late afternoon light. Our fear was palpable and felt unspeakable. We were all somewhat frozen. Our guide, Ron, noticed our fear, and reflected it back to us. He spoke a bit about fear and then suggested we stand together in a circle and speak our fears into the center of the circle. The air was quiet and heavy for several moments. Then as we quietly began to name our fears and began to release the tension, our voices grew stronger and the energy got lighter. We all spoke our fears aloud at the same time into the circle. As we let go of our tension, we discovered we could be present to ourselves and to each other. Fear had temporarily lost its stranglehold on our experience. We learned we had similar fears and that by sharing them, we were released and connected at the same time. We could move into the experience of the sweat lodge with openness.

In another situation, I learned about fear while traveling in Copper Canyon Mexico with a group of elders. The local shaman said as he looked into my eyes, that I was scared inside and that the scare needed to come out. He did not tell anyone else this. I felt embarrassed and ashamed. Ron, our guide, gave me a powerful gift. He said we all have fear. He suggested that I might want to carry the experience as a meditation for the remainder of the quest. I learned that fear is often present and that I can carry it with me as I move forward toward my dreams. I can breathe into my fear and learn to stay present. I can tell someone I am afraid. The fear does not stop me or shut me down. I just need to acknowledge and accept it.

ASSORTED THOUGHTS ON AGING

I love what Carolyn Heilbrun suggests in *Writing a Woman's Life*: as we get older, we can claim freedom from being a female impersonator and from fulfilling the needs of others. What a great relief to give up the beauty game. To dress and look as I want to, not to impress or compete. My children are grown, my husband is self-sufficient and I choose friends who have clear boundaries and are full of life energy. I feel more balanced and serene than ever before in my life. Now I want to give myself to something bigger than myself, something to the community.

When I was fifty years old and menopausal, I began designing and facilitating workshops for women on the topic of menopause. What a great learning that was for me. The women in the classes shared their experiences and wisdom and we all learned together that menopause is a natural transition in a woman's life made easier by sharing it with each other.

Living in a misogynist culture where the powerful

feminine is greatly feared, we continually discover that as women, we need each other to help us voice our own truth.

Few women think of old age and power as compatible ideas, especially in the United States. Women's empowerment needs to continue on into our elder years. We have to tell each other the way it really is growing older. As Maxine Kumin suggests, we need new kinds of consciousness-raising for our elder years. This time we need to challenge the negative stereotypes of older women. We can help each other name the possibilities we hardly recognize or dare to put a name to. We need each other as aging women to help us affirm and express our radical and radiant inner self that seems to carry the mystery and meaning of our life. Finding a community where we can tell our story, explore our fears and strengths, harvest and claim the wisdom we have learned from living our life seems essential. This has always been a way women have given voice to themselves and as Nelle Morton observes, heard each other into being and power. It is time to continue that process into the elder years and share our bounty with the younger women.

It seems to me we have a choice. We can view aging as a catastrophe and disintegration, focusing on the aches and pains and losses (and they are there and that is true) but that is not all there is. Aging can also be viewed as an adventure. Remember Lillian Carter who joined the Peace Corps at sixty-eight? I believe it is vital for me to find meaning in my elder years beyond family, in a larger community. Sitting in a circle of women over sixty years of age, sharing what makes each of us feel connected to life, practices that nourish our spirits, and contemplating Mary Oliver's question, which I have paraphrased, "Tell me what is it you plan to do with the rest of your one wild and precious life?"[8] I want to continue to live the passionate life, to savor the preciousness of these years, and I want the company of other thoughtful women to accompany me on this journey.

THOUGHTS ON
AGING MINDFULLY

2010

There is no old age. There is, as there always was, just you.
—CAROL MATTHAU, quoted by Oprah Winfrey,
    O Magazine

In the past fifteen years, I have discovered a great treasure for my elder years. It is in women's circles that I want to share my gifts and energy. It is also a place I come to be restored.

I come to Pelican House in January this year to write about my personal experience of aging and what it might mean to age mindfully. As I contemplate turning seventy, I am looking back at my life as I look forward to my remaining years. The most obvious truth is that the years left to me are fewer and precious. I find that the same questions I asked at puberty and menopause, I began contemplating again in my sixties: Who am I? What is important to me now? What gives my life meaning? What do I love? Now that I have again spent time with these questions, I feel quite clear in my answers. In my seventies, new questions have arisen: How and where do I want to spend my energy and share my gifts? What restores my energy now? What are the life lessons I have learned and want to share? How do I want to prepare for my death?

Balancing time for solitude and reflection with time for social activities is an ongoing challenge. For the past two years, my focus has been on deepening my relationships with myself, with loved ones, with the natural world, and with the Divine. I am learning to practice slowing. It is easier to slow down here at Pelican House than at home. This year I discover that giving myself the gift of deep rest first helps everything else unfold. I notice that that I love long quiet mornings sitting in bed eating breakfast, drinking coffee, journaling and reading. I enjoy walking the beach, appreciating how the light sparkles on the water and illuminates the air. I take deep breaths and fill my chest with living air. I pray for illumination. Some days, I spend hours exploring the maritime forest trails. After two days of naps and rest, I begin writing for a few hours each day. The highlight of each day at Pelican House is our evening circle. After a full day of delicious silence in the house, we women gather in a circle of soft chairs around a central altar of candles and sacred objects. We dim the lights, place more candles around the room and wrap ourselves in our scarves and blankets.

Backlit by the flames of a fire in the fireplace, we settle into ourselves and a long sweet winter's evening of sharing stories of our day, our ponderings, our writing and poetry, our feelings and creations. As the bells ring to close our circle, we sit in the delicious silence. We are hesitant to leave the nurturing warmth of our circle of sisters and the wise loving presence that surrounds us.

As a young girl, I felt most at home in the forest and along and in the river. I spent ten summers of my youth living in a small rustic cabin on the banks of the Delaware River in rural northeastern Pennsylvania. Lying on the forest floor, walking for hours alone in the woods, jumping from rock to rock amidst the rapids, sitting in the sun and shade dreaming, adopting a dairy cow for the summer, playing house in a rhododendron thicket, catching frogs and putting them to bed in carefully-crafted canopied Velveeta boxes, taming a wild barn cat to lie on my lap for belly rubs, adventuring downstream on the river in a handmade wooden rowboat and then rowing back against the current, learning to swim the river's width against the current—these memories bring delight and insight to me now. Throughout my adulthood, I have enjoyed camping and sailing. I still do. I continue to spend time each week walking and exploring the local forest trails and streams near my home. I invite my grandchildren on hikes and speak to them of the tiny fairies, gnomes, and magical beings that live in the little hobbit houses along the trail. I walk with beloved friends who also know the forest as their soul's home. I occasionally consider getting trained as a vision quest guide and offering local programs in the state.

Here at Pelican House, I walk amid the dancing trees of the maritime forest and by the waters of the sound and ocean feeling deeply nourished and delighted by what I discover. On a Vision Quest about six years ago, while sitting on the ground in the high canyonlands of Utah for three days and nights, fasting, alone and exposed to the elements, I heard and sensed the Earth speak to me and claim me. She said, "This is where you belong"…she held me in my exhaustion, my loneliness and fear. A consistent thread throughout my life is a deep visceral appreciation of the natural world as a beautiful nurturing home. One of my worries now is imagining a time when I can no longer go to the woods and walk freely. I know that time will come. In the meantime, I go as often as I want and relish each soul-enhancing encounter. I exercise regularly to maintain my strength and flexibility. I breathe in the stars on a cold night and twirl in the wind on the beach. I thank the trees, the flowers and the creatures for their wise presence and gifts.

Another major thread woven through my life is an appreciation and love for my sensuous female body. As a girl, I loved the feel of water on my skin, of shampooing my hair in the river and diving down to the cooler deep layers of the river to rinse out the soap. I remember the tingle of foaming bubbles in the surf on my skin and how I would gather a handful of foam and rub it on my face. At the age of eight, I spent Saturday mornings in a vacant lot at the end of my street. I would ride a young bent-over tree as if it was my horse. I rode that horse for miles across the wild western plains of my imagination. One day, I found a dead rabbit by my horse-tree and removed the soft cottontail carrying it home. My mother and father were horrified when I brought it into the house, stroking it on my cheek. Despite their horror, I managed to save it for years. Eating blackberries warmed by the sun, smelling pungent cow manure in the pasture, feeling myself respond to beautiful music, all resonated in my body. As a young woman, I loved all the fantastic body sensations of "making out." As a grown woman, I enjoyed making love, breastfeeding my babies, the feel of my children's bare skin on mine and the smell of their sweet bodies. In midlife, when my children were grown, I discovered massage and for several years while I was working, I had a massage once a month.

Now as my body changes with rows of puckered skin on my arms and legs, deepening wrinkle lines on my face, loose skin on my neck, drooping breasts, the loss of my waist (that happened twenty years ago), and the beginnings of the protruding belly of old age, I continue to love the feel of skin on skin and the delicious experience of eros. My body continues to resonate with my surroundings and serves as a source of wisdom. When the palms of my hands and soles of my feet burn, I know my heart is open and healing energy is present. I have thought maybe I would like to learn more about energy work for healing and offer touch for health. I want to be involved in something where I can give myself away and use my talents. I have time and flexibility. At the same time, I want to maintain some freedom after years of childrearing and working. But I am willing to give up some of that freedom for the joy of working in areas where learning and teaching are combined.

I realize that I have less energy than ten years ago and I am not willing nor can I push myself and get the results I want. Pushing and forcing simply do not work anymore. Deep rest and nourishing silence give me creative energy and restore my connection to the inner teacher. This week at Pelican House, I have given myself permission to nap, relax, and be quiet. I brought art materials to make a visioning board for 2010, but am carrying it all back home unopened. I know that simplifying and prioritizing are essential daily tools. I do not want to spend my best energy on household tasks, like laundry, food shopping, and cooking. I do not want to spend these precious years taking care of "objects and things." I want to take time each morning to ask myself the vital questions: What does my soul want and need today? What is the best use of my time right now? I pray for divine guidance as I spiral within and without.

I pay more attention to synchronicity. In recent conversations with several different groups and individuals, the topic of aging arises. I am hungry to have meaningful conversations about what we are experiencing as we retire from the highly structured work world and search for meaning and purpose in our daily lives. I believe the experience of aging has much to teach us. As we pay full attention to our changing and deepening values, many of us choose to live in ways that run counter to our culture of unconscious consumption and the intensity of the fast lane. In the small groups I have led entitled, "Women Over Sixty" and "Wise Choices," participants expressed a desire for more solitude and time for quiet reflection. As we learn to slow down, be quiet and listen, we begin to see things as they are. We live more mindfully. We recalibrate our intentions and refocus our energies. We move into our experience, paying attention and learning as we go. We create our own internal maps and our inner guide. When I first entered my sixties, I was intensely aware that there were no maps or guides to this new territory. As we navigate it and share our stories, we all learn. New possibilities arise and we grow in wisdom. We may discover our deepest needs are for community and deep relationships, compassion, simple living in sync with the natural world and a grace-filled faith.

STORY BY THE FIRE, THE POWER OF CIRCLES

[Previously published in Conscious Living, Conscious Aging by Ron Pevny.]

When I was in my midlife and going through menopause, I had experiences with doctors and other healthcare professionals that left me confused and frustrated. I did not believe I needed drugs or hormone replacement therapy (HRT) to be healthy, and I was concerned about the side effects. I told my doctor my concerns about HRT and that I would not be following his advice for now. His irritated, dismissive response left me determined to learn as much as I possibly could about healthy menopause.

I began by attending lectures by women physicians and reading medical literature, which was depressing. They put a disease spin on a normal life transition. All the words were about disintegration, deterioration, disease, and loss, while I was feeling vibrant, healthy, and strong. The mismatch between the medical model and my experience was glaring. I readjusted my search to books supporting a focus on creating health and wellness during menopause. The information in these few resources was enough to create a framework for a workshop series I developed and led at Duke University through the employee wellness department, where I had been leading health promotion programs for several years. Sixteen women gathered in a circle during the lunch hour once a week for four weeks. As I listened to the participants speak of their experiences and discover their knowing, I often felt chills run up one side of my body and down the other. What happened in this group led to the creation of many "healthy menopause" circles over the next ten years.

What most struck me about these groups is that women usually showed up the first time filled with fear. Woman after woman said that her body felt out of control, as I had felt when I first made an appointment with the doctor. As we told our stories, we discovered that we were not alone, which greatly reduced our fear and stress. In listening to ways others found to cope with their challenges, we found creative ways to cope with our own. In the safety of the group, we gradually spoke of our vulnerabilities, strengths, and yearnings. The depth of sharing and compassion the women had for themselves and each other gave us all courage to speak from deeper parts of ourselves, connect our perceptions, and create meaning out of our suffering. We began to define for ourselves the meaning of our midlife experience.

When I entered my sixties, I once again felt like I was walking into unfamiliar territory without a map or guide. I signed up to participate in a conscious eldering rite of passage program and experienced the powerful process of council—speaking from the heart, listening with the ears of the heart, and being aware of the impact of our words on the group. These guidelines, along with Christina Baldwin's circle basics described in her book *Calling the Circle,* became the foundation for my future work as an elder. As I recalled my experience with midlife groups, I decided to offer "women over sixty" circles to explore the possibilities, challenges, and gifts of aging. To explore conscious aging, we need both solitude and community to help us listen to our deeper selves and discover our personal truths. We create a circle to support the internal journey of each person, a circle that helps them feel safe enough to develop a relationship with their inner wisdom. In the circle we also learn from each other. We practice presence.

As I move into my seventies, I continue to seek sacred

circles where my soul will feel safe enough to speak out and I will have the gift of hearing others' souls speak—in places where elders may mirror and support each other, places where they can reflect and shine their light on the inner light of others, midwifing inner wisdom. In circle, in community, we find companions to journey with through our elder years. We help each other make meaning of our life experience and discover the wisdom we want to pass on to future generations. We support each other in taking meaningful action in the world.

TURNING POINTS

I am devoted to the process of women's sacred circles and the power of shared stories to create meaningful feminine medicine for the world. After participating in three intergenerational women's retreats, I wanted to gather a group of women of different ages to write about turning points in their lives in a workshop writing series. The hope was, as we reflected and studied our own experiences, and gave voice to our stories and were witnessed, that all of us would be enriched.

So, I went to Jeanette Stokes, who introduced me to Rebecca Welper, a gifted writer and leader of writing groups through the Resource Center for Women and Ministry in the South. Together we planned a four-part series focused on the turning points in our lives as they related to the life stages of the Triple Goddess: Maiden, Mother, and Crone aspects of the feminine present in all of us, regardless of age.

Due to the generosity of the participants and the skill and diligence of Rebecca and Jeanette, we have created a small booklet, *Turning Points,* of our writings to share with others.

[Anita wrote the following two reflections for *Turning Points.*]

A CHANGE IN FERTILITY

Loss of fertility does not mean loss of desire and fulfillment. But it does entail a change, a change involving matters even more important—if I may venture a heresy—than sex.

The woman who is willing to make that change must become pregnant with herself, at last.

—URSULA K. LEGUIN, *Dancing at the Edge of the World*

The change is taking a long time. It is slow going and requires focus and effort. Slowing down feels like a major change in fertility as I withdraw from the extroverted activities related to the outside world. I am a natural planner and organizer and I feel awkward limiting my attention to my inner process. I want to focus on my interior images and explore my inner world. At first I felt dry and barren, then restless and impatient. I asked myself what the hell was I doing! I want to do what I have always done, what feels familiar, engaging and safe. Come on, I say to myself, lighten up; this could be interesting. A new expanded story, a new way of being, go somewhere else inside and embrace the questions within. Remember, I say to myself, the answers of value are within, not in the stack of books on my desk, bedside table and on the floor. Trust. . . . trust yourself. It takes time and patience to listen and be present.

CRONE

As a crone I reject and despise the culturally widespread caricature of old women as ugly and evil. As a crone, I intend to live from the inside out. I intend to inhabit myself and my knowing. I hope to be outrageous, irreverent and whimsical. I want to learn the deep mysteries of nature and tell the truth with humor and grace. I want to walk barefoot in the grass, sleep in the forest, sing to the birds and care for the children and community. As a crone, I plan to continue to hang out with other crones and make trouble for the patriarchy. I hope and pray to deepen my inner learning so I have something of value to share with others. Growing a garden, being outdoors in the natural world, tending, teaching and living as part of the sacred universe with others of all ages is of high value to me. I intend to deepen my practice of prayer and creating rituals to bring the Feminine Divine back into our daily lives.

WRITING ON A MOUNTAIN

Retreat at Hound Ears
Three words: peace, peaceful, cabins

I am reminded of the mountain cabins of my childhood. I remember how content and adventuresome I felt as a girl in the mountains of northeastern Pennsylvania. Now when I think about the mountains and walking the trails through the dense green forests, I experience a deep sense of peace that moves through and fills my body. There is a peacefulness that is present and palpable when I am in the mountains. Something deep and nourishing fills my soul as I inhale the quiet moist greenness. I look at the rounded uprising of the earth and know these hills have been here for thousands of years. They are a product of glacial movement, earthquakes, water, wind and other mystical forces of nature. That is the big picture. And then there are all the creatures that find a home here. From the tree families to the communities of plants, insects, birds and animal beings living together in harmonic diversity. Could we humans learn from the natural world how to live together in peace? Could we discover and remember that the earth with her mountains, valleys and waters sustains our very life? Can we remember our souls are connected to the Great Soul of our Mother, the Earth? Maybe if more people climbed to the top of a mountain, they would have a wider, longer, and deeper view and would catch a glimpse of the peace that is possible. Like Martin

Luther King, Jr., who said he had been to the mountaintop and was inspired and filled and forever changed.

ELLEN

I want to tell you what I remember about Ellen. When I think back fifty-five years, I can still see her bright twinkling green-hazel eyes, light brown fine hair, her face dusted with honey-colored freckles and the wide smile of an impish young girl. We were in school together since first grade. In grammar school, everyone walked home for lunch except for those few children whose mothers worked. They brought their lunch to school in brown paper sacks and bought milk in the auditorium where they were taken to eat. There were no lunchrooms or cafeterias in our school. On a few occasions in the fourth and fifth grade I remember Ellen came home with me to eat lunch. It was a special occasion because she is the only friend I remember eating lunch with me at my house in grammar school. Now I wonder what that was about. Why were my friends not welcome?

Ellen lived about two miles from school. She lived with her grandmother, her parents had left her there, she said. She occasionally heard from her mother on her birthday, but never got to see her or talk to her. I always thought that was so sad and I could not imagine how it would feel to live like that. She said her grandmother was mean and punished her regularly. I cannot remember details, but I do recall her saying she was often locked in her room and not allowed to go out. She did not have many clothes and sometimes she smelled like she hadn't had a bath in a while or was wearing dirty clothes. I never went in the house she lived in. I only stood outside at the gate and waited for her to come out. When we played together nearby in the graveyard of the Dutch Reformed Church across the railroad tracks, Colleen often joined us. We would chase each other through the graveyard, being careful not to step on the graves. The church was an old brick and stone structure surrounded by gnarled trees, appearing gothic and mysterious in the dim light of evening. We would chase and hide and jump out at each other from behind the trees and the moss-covered cement benches on the church grounds, squealing with fear and delighting in our bravery. We pretended and believed, as eight-year-old girls can, that ghosts and spirits were lurking about. We ran and we screamed and we secretly delighted in our bravery. We were a wild threesome. Colleen lived down the street from Ellen. I did go to her house for her birthday once. I remember we played a game naming the forty-eight states and their capitols. Ellen was not there because she was supposedly sick. I think Colleen and I knew it was her mean old grandmother who would not let her come and have cake, ice cream and some fun!

One Friday after school in the fifth grade, the three of us decided to carry out a plan we had been hatching for weeks. When the school bell rang at the end of the day, we ran as fast as we could up tree-lined Prospect Avenue, turned right on to Edgewater Road by St. Matthews Catholic Church, went across an alley, and snuck into the bushes bordering the

Jacoby land. Mr. Jacoby lived alone in a large hundred-year-old Victorian mansion that looked exactly like a haunted house, with peeling paint, broken front steps, dirty gray gingerbread trim that hadn't been painted in years, and large windows on the second floor bordered by loose hanging shutters. Two hundred yards behind this house was a large dilapidated barn, once painted white to match the house, but now in a state of disrepair. I think the story was that a very wealthy Jacoby family had lived there before the turn of the century, but had lost their fortune in the Great Depression.

Ellen, Colleen, and I wanted to explore the barn. We had scouted the place on several Saturdays and discovered that while the barn doors were padlocked, a window was slightly open on the west side. That was to be our point of entry. The house and field looked deserted and there were no cars or trucks parked nearby, so we crept up to the barn window carrying cinder blocks we had placed in the bushes earlier. We stacked the blocks, pushed the window open wide enough so we three, one at a time, could climb inside. What we saw first took our breath away! It was a large dark red antique horse-drawn sleigh with leather bridle straps and a harness trimmed with sleigh bells. Dusty fur wraps were piled on the cracked black leather seats. It looked just like the horse-drawn sleighs pictured on Christmas cards. We were speechless at first and then delighted to pieces! We had found hidden treasure and our eight-year-old girl selves were ecstatic.

We ran around the first floor of the barn uncovering one

discovery after another—old musty books, rusted pitchforks, multiple tools, and large shipping chests once used for ocean travel. We carefully crept up the rickety stairs to the second floor to see what else we might find. There were stacks of baled hay, more tools and not much else of interest.

When Ellen, Colleen and I looked out the second story loft window of the old barn and saw Mr. Jacoby striding across the field toward us carrying a rifle in his right hand, we knew we had to run like the wind or our lives would be changed forever. Panic hit, we had to get out of there! As we scrambled to reach the stairs, Ellen's foot went through the flooring into the insulation and she started crying "my grandmother will kill me for getting my socks dirty." Colleen and I grabbed her, pulled her foot out and told her to get moving fast before Mr. Jacoby shot us. We clambered down the stairs and Colleen helped Ellen out the window. I then hoisted Colleen up, she jumped out of the window and then I climbed up and out. I was the tallest so I went last. We ran across the grass field to the bushes, our point of entry, then split up without talking and each of us ran to her own home. I was terrified and I was exhilarated. We had not been shot, we got away and we had seen the horse-drawn Christmas sleigh in Jacoby's old barn.

The following morning my mother read out loud an article in the local newspaper about hoodlums that had broken into the Jacoby property. The police were investigating. She read that the robbers had entered through an open window on the west side of the barn and the blood left my head as I wondered if the police would find our fingerprints and arrest us. Of course, I did not tell my parents or anyone and suffered several sleepless nights. Colleen, Ellen and I kept our secret adventure to ourselves. A fearless threesome of eight-year-old girls could imagine and carry out an escapade that made headlines in the local newspaper and still keep their secret fifty years later. The mystery remains unsolved.

When Colleen, Ellen and I became adolescents, we lost touch with each other. In junior high school, our class size increased fivefold and we were by then on different educational tracks. When we entered high school, we were bused to a regional school of about seven hundred students and rarely passed each other in the hallways.

So, at the age of fifteen, when I heard that Ellen had died of suicide and that her funeral was to be in two days, memories of our girlhood adventures came into my mind and I knew I had to go. Our classmates said she didn't have many friends. I wondered who her friends were and if her parents would be there.

Who wouldn't wail and sob and scream with grief at the sight of a fifteen-year-old freckle-faced girl with rope marks on her neck from hanging herself? Who could possibly look at her and not shed a tear? What kind of inhumanness would that require? What is so terrifying about expressing grief? Why are we called upon to act like robots in times of great loss? It seems unbelievably cruel to expect loving human beings to be quiet in their grief. There needs to be freedom to wail. We shouldn't have to go into a closed private space to weep so as to not upset others. Suffering is relieved by sharing, not by bearing our sorrow in silence. I wonder if most of us in this culture find it so hard to be with suffering because we have not expressed our own sorrow, we have pushed it down like I have and are afraid if we start letting it go, we will not be able to stop!

SAYING GOODBYE TO SID

2004

It is an evening in January 2004 and the wind is biting cold and fierce. It howls and screams in the darkness around the windows, eaves and crevices of a funeral home in Creedmoor, North Carolina. I walk up to the door—it takes much of my strength to open it against the wind—and walk inside. As the door closes behind me, the first thing I notice is a sweet smell. The heavy sweet smell is of dead roses, or gladiolas, or maybe a perfumed spray that hangs thickly in the air, conjuring up images of other times in places like this, places of grief and death and suffering. I want to run from the building, but I do not because I am a grown-up now. I take a deep breath through my mouth, reach for my husband's hand and look around. We are at the end of a long line of men and women gathered to pay their respects to Sid Oakley, the husband of my dear friend, Pat.

I lower my eyes and examine the clumps of wet dirty snow and mud tracked onto the dusty rose carpet by the mourners. The side tables lining the long hallway hold a variety of dead plastic flower arrangements. I wish the flowers were alive. I wish they were fresh sunflowers. I wish there were abundant groupings of sunflowers strewn everywhere. They were Sid's favorite flower and he enjoyed painting them. I wish I had thought to bring a huge bunch of them tonight!

To distract myself from the penetrating odor, I look around to see who is here. There must be more than two hundred people. Some of the men are clad in denim overalls and wool shirts buttoned up against the cold winter wind. Others are in dark suits and ties. Some of these suited men have come straight from work and this is what they wear every day. Others have gone to great effort to dress up in their Sunday best suits and neckties after a day's hard physical labor. A faint scent of Old Spice lingers in the air around them.

Some of the women are wearing church dresses and high heels, others are in pants or long flowing skirts. I notice one woman with long gray hair down to her hips, another with short spiky hair. There are also the men and women in black—black pants, coats and shoes—people who wear black as a uniform every day. Some folks are elders, but there are many young people here as well.

Standing directly in front of me is a massive thirty-something man with legs like tree trunks and a back as wide as a barn door dressed in a dark suit that feels ready to split at the seams. His shiny curly dark hair is pulled into a ponytail barely contained by a rubber band. His dark beard is thick and carefully sculpted. I want to lean my body into him. I imagine how comforting it would feel to be sheltered by his arms of mighty oak. I allow myself to drift into a lusty fantasy, enjoying the heat rising in my body and the warm flush in my cheeks.

More people join the line behind us—quietly talking, laughing, people greeting each other. I do not know anyone here so far and think, This is going to take longer, much longer, than I imagined.

Sid's life seems well represented here tonight. There are people from widely diverse backgrounds and lifestyles—potters, farmers, doctors, poets, lawyers, authors, and business people. People loved Sid because he was always ready for conversation and prided himself as a nurturer and mentor of his friends' talents.

HOMILY FOR ELIZABETH AND DELOIS

September 2001

I would like to share a few words with you on this your wedding day. The fact that you purposely chose this day, the day of the autumn equinox when day and night are in balance on the earth and the harvest is being celebrated, speaks volumes about the intent of your relationship.

You each come from families that love you, from friendships that have touched you deeply. You now bring your individual strengths and treasures as well as your wounds and limitations to each other and to the sacred covenant of marriage. I would like to offer you some words of encouragement. Much of this you know, but I feel it bears repeating and reminding.

First of all, it is obvious both from your wedding vows and from spending time with the two of you over this past year that you are aware of the importance of nurturing your relationship with your inner selves. You have promised in your vows to deepen your own uniqueness and to listen to your own inner source of wisdom. I strongly encourage you to remember each and every day to renew your solitude. For it is in filling yourself that you can give to each other out of your own abundance.

Second, your relationship itself is a living, striving organism. It has its own timing, sense of balance and destination. It will carry you along with it where it needs to go. From the moment you pledge yourselves to each other unconditionally, much will change. For example, as you make a home, ancient gods and demons of your childhood will return to live with you, challenging you to grow and trust. Begin with the knowledge that you will often fail each other. A thousand times you will forget to listen, tread roughly on sacred ground, reopen each other's ancient wounds, say too much or too little, and more. You can keep your love alive by practicing the art of forgiveness. Your love can remain vital if you forgive each other a thousand and one times. And begin again. So tend the sanctuary of your relationship with frequent attention. Strive to balance the dark with the light, and seriousness with play. More than anything, the marriage relationship can be how we heal ourselves and each other.

And finally, as you seek to balance between cherishing yourselves and caring for your relationship, know that marriage is a spiritual enterprise. It calls for a process of transformation. Marriage is the spiritual grinding stone that can hone you to your brightest brilliance. It will cause you to become not only who you want to be, but also the person who you have no choice but to be. In marriage you will be changed, for in choosing this particular person to love and make your whole life with, you are choosing to be affected. Remember that what inspires you now about your partner will at times in the future irritate you, drawing you into a journey of personal evolution.

This is a spiritual process because it deals with the deepest essence of being and, ultimately, with your capacity to love. You will learn to be kinder and more gently critical, to be empathetic and more trusting. For wherever you are bound by limitations or held back by your own woundedness, you will be met in marriage with an invitation to move forward and reach for your capacity to love. For it is love, unconditional love, the love of the tree for the earth, the love of the birds for the air, the love of the Creator for creation, which shatters all limitations and dissolves all fears. This unconditional love is the true and sacred gift of marriage. You cannot will it with your mind; you grow into it with your heart, as your heart breaks open over and over and you fall back into love again and again. May this gift be yours.

SECTION IV

REFLECTIONS ON ANITA

ANITA'S REMARKABLE, CREATIVE, and inspiring life was celebrated in January 2017 at Eno River Unitarian Universalist Fellowship in Durham. Her dear friends Jeanette Stokes, Debra Brazzel, and Martha Abshire Simmons offered their remembrances, as did Anita's beloved son Scott. Several months later, on what would have been Anita's 78th birthday, her husband Mike shared further remarks.

A MEMORIAL SERVICE AND CELEBRATION OF LIFE

~~~~~~~~~~~~~~~~~~~~~~~~~~~~~~~~

Anita Swensen McLeod
January 16, 2017
Eno River Unitarian Universalist Fellowship

A TRIBUTE TO ANITA MCLEOD
The Rev. Jeanette Stokes

My job is to explain what Anita was doing when she was not with her family.

The poet Mary Oliver has written:

> When death comes . . .
> I don't want to end up simply having visited this world.[9]

Last week, in looking for pictures of Anita—on my phone, on my computer, and in old photo albums at our office—I was overwhelmed by what I found. As we know, Anita was bright, beautiful, and funny. There she was laughing, leading, and loving people, but what surprised me was that she was also ubiquitous. She was always there.

I met Anita 20 years ago in a yearlong class on women and spirituality at Duke Divinity School. Several of you were in that class. In the next few years after that, Anita and I taught a course for Duke Continuing Education on the same topic: women and spirituality. And after that, she began to design and lead circles, classes, and retreats of her own for the Resource Center for Women and Ministry in the South, which I direct.

As I looked at pictures of Anita, I noticed that without calling attention to herself, she was always there. She joined our board of trustees and eventually served as the chair of the board. She came to book readings, lectures, and workshops other people led. She was central to our 25th Anniversary celebration in 2002 and to our exhibition a few years later called "Art and the Feminine Divine."

Anita's way of being in the world was a perfect match for the vision of the Resource Center. We are in the business of empowering women to weave feminism and spirituality into a vision of justice in the world. That is what Anita was about. She supported the Resource Center and the Resource Center supported her. We provided the platform or stage on which she could do what she loved most—teach and lead and empower others. And she did it brilliantly.

She was the group leader I trusted the most. I was confident that she could handle anyone or anything that might come up. After working with surly, hungry clients at Structure House and Duke's Live for Life programs, a few upset women in a small group did not scare Anita McLeod.

When I counted the number of events Anita had either initiated or led for us over the last fifteen years, the list got longer and longer. Fifty events. She led or organized fifty events for us. She was always there.

Anita embodied feminist principles in her leadership style: she trusted groups of women to learn from and teach one another without her having to be the kind of teacher who tells participants everything they need to know. She trusted the groups more than the "experts."

She invented classes, workshops, and ongoing groups on topics she wanted to learn more about. She began with Menopause and moved on to Mothers and Daughters, Women over Sixty, Wise Choices, intergenerational writing workshops, workshops about the natural world (such as When Grandmothers Speak, the Earth Will Heal), and finally end-of-life issues and Befriending Death.

The last ones make me wonder. Did she know? Did she have some inkling that the coins left in her purse were numbered? Did she know that she needed to befriend the end of life? We will never know, but what she taught and learned served her well. She approached these last two months with an open heart and with her insatiable curiosity. And she was not afraid.

But now she is gone. Or is she? The poet Kahlil Gibran has written:

> Close your eyes and you will see me with you
> forevermore. . . .
> Go back to the joy of your dwellings and you will
> find there
> That which Death cannot remove from you and
> me.[10]

In the last months of her life, when reflecting on what she was learning in her dying, she said, "I don't know how to explain it, but this is not about me! This is for the world. Please don't let them make this only about me."

So if this is not just about Anita but is also about us, what would Anita want for us to do now? I think that with the prophet she would want us to do justice, to love kindness, and to be decent companions for all the creatures of the world.

In December, she wrote her last email to the mailing list of the Resource Center for Women and Ministry in the South (RCWMS). She said: "The Divine Feminine is with us as lover and warrior. She is calling elder women to stand up for the precious earth and water and creatures. For ourselves. For our children."

I think Anita would want us to walk in the woods, to keep our friends and loved ones close, to march in Raleigh and in Washington, and to speak up on behalf of vulnerable people, vulnerable creatures, and the earth.

In order to do that, we are going to have to resist some pretty strong forces in this country. I've been saying I've never been an obstructionist before, but in the current political climate, I think I'm going to enjoy being one. And I'm certain Anita will be right there: resisting, rejoicing, and cheering us on.

HOMILY

The Rev. Debra Brazzel

It has been one of the great gifts of my life to know and love Anita McLeod for more than twenty-two years. Many of you have loved her even longer! She has been essential in my life. With Martha Simmons, I was co-teaching that first women's spirituality class when Anita cracked us open and changed us from strangers to soul sisters by speaking truth with raw vulnerability and power. She did that every time we met over the next two decades. With Anita I always felt seen, accepted and loved. That is why the grief runs so deep. I know many of you feel the same way.

Over the past two months, we have been hurting. We have been in disbelief at how quickly Anita's life and, with her, our lives changed. I spent time with Anita in the mountains and at the beach in October with our women's circles.

Two weeks after that, she was diagnosed with a brain tumor. After she got sick, I expected Anita to beat it because, well, she was Anita, the most "super" woman I have ever known. Even two weeks ago when I first saw her after the surgery, I thought we would have more time. I know many of you are in various stages of grief. Our grief is a reflection of the depth of our love and that makes it a blessing. The loss is great but so are the love and gratitude.

On behalf of the McLeod family, I thank you for your outpouring of love and support—the cards and comments on CaringBridge, the meals, the offers to do something, anything, to show how much you care, have meant a lot.

We all wanted more time with Anita. We needed to see her one more time, to tell her how much we love her and value her and need her still. I want you to know that she knew and received all that love, even if you weren't able to tell her in person.

I also want to thank the McLeod family, and especially Mike, for sharing Anita with us through the years. How many women's circles did you host? How many times did you have to find someplace to go hang out and then come back and we were still there! How many classes and work- shops and retreats did Anita take or lead? You shared her and we are so grateful for that time. And over the past eight weeks, when you've had to face her unimaginable illness and prepare for her death, you still made space to receive our of- ferings and grief, even in the midst of your own. Chris, I know that managing all that was almost a fulltime job! We thank you for opening your hearts to us.

Mike has given me permission to share some of their experiences these past few weeks. Anita faced her illness with extraordinary courage. She was diagnosed on a Friday and had an open craniotomy just a few days later. It wasn't that there was no fear, but Anita faced down the fear, refusing to let fear determine her journey. Anita chose to be awake and participate in her surgery to preserve as much of her movement, speech and consciousness as possible. She accepted her diagnosis and said, "This is my path to walk now." And Mike said, "I will walk it with you to the end, however you choose." And he did. Mike and Anita's love for each other was fierce and beautiful to witness.

Because of her work in conscious aging and befriending death, Anita had clarity about what she wanted. Last spring, long before her diagnosis, she asked me to lead her memorial service when the time came. Of course, I said, I would be honored in ten years, twenty years, never expecting we would lose her so soon! Anita had advance directives. She made clear choices. When the tumor returned, she chose to end debilitating chemotherapy and return to her home of fifty years. At home, she was lovingly tended in her solarium so she could look out at nature. Her energy came back and she was able to gather her children and grandchildren to say goodbye. She kept her sense of humor, greeting her grandchildren from Nebraska with Groucho Marx glasses and nose and mustache. Their Gigi was changed but she was still the Gigi they loved

Throughout her illness, Anita was learning and teaching. She healed old wounds around her mother's death from a brain tumor. She reconnected with her nursing career and befriended every person who tended her. She told me she felt so much exuberance that she would forget her body wasn't up for holding all that joy.

When Anita made the decision to come home, she made sure that all the words that needed to be spoken were said. About two weeks ago, she invited me to meet with her and Mike and their children to share memories for her memorial service. Usually stories are told later, if at all, but Anita didn't want to miss out on anything! As we sat together in her beautiful solarium she and her children told stories to much laughter and tears. We celebrated their life together right then! It was brilliant and totally Anita!

Here are a few of the stories Anita wanted shared:

If you read Anita's obituary you already know about the importance of their odyssey to California. Picture Anita and Mike in the '70s, four children between the ages of seven and thirteen, an eighty-pound lab, a yellow Suburban, a small camper and bicycles. One month camping across country each way. Arriving in Marin County with no place to live. Finding a small two-bedroom apartment with what the kids describe as prison bunk beds. In self-defense, Scott moved a mattress under the stairs. There was rented furniture, no TV, six forks and six plastic plates. They were minimalists, ahead of their time! Everybody had a night to cook, even the seven-year-old. There was no washer and dryer and whenever Mike went to the laundromat, the kids said he was too cheap to dry the clothes all the way. They would complain to Anita about their wet jeans and she would say, "talk to your father." Every weekend, they loaded the Suburban and camper and took off, up and down the coast making memories that have endured a lifetime.

This move came at a time when Mike and Anita were renegotiating their relationship, not the last time they did that hard work. With courage, they threw out the mold that no longer worked and made a new one. Everyone described the "before California" and "after California" parents. BC Mike was white button down shirts and ties. AC Mike was beard and turtlenecks. BC Anita was heels and dresses. AC Anita (to Chris' mortification) was hairy legs and Birkenstocks. She remembers saying, "Mom, please don't wear that to the PTA!", which Anita, of course, ignored.

Mike and Anita forged a strong marriage because they were willing to change. Later there were couples' groups. Mike remembers asking why they had to do that when other couples didn't. The kids remember asking whether other parents had foam bats! The point is they believed they were worth the effort. In the '80s they bought a small condo at the beach so they could have alone time. Then they bought their beloved sailboat "Free to Be" that Anita called their sacred temple. They co-captained the boat with Anita taking her own class in learning how to be the captain! Few people were ever invited onto that boat. Anita would say, "Your Dad and I need some soft belly time." In their fifty-five years of marriage their love was tested, strengthened, and refined to pure gold. Toward the end, Anita told Mike, "This is what the vows are about. You get a gold star." They promised to show up for each other and stay in the present moment and love, love, love.

The relationship they modeled is one of the things their children most appreciate about Anita and Mike: their true partnership, their willingness to do the hard work, the effort and money they invested in strengthening relationships and creating lasting memories with family trips all over the country, especially Mexico and the trip for Mike's eightieth birthday. Anita and Mike always drew their family into nature and invited them to notice the beauty all around them. Their children have tried to do the same with their own children.

Anita and Mike also knew how to thread the needle between being engaged and overbearing grandparents. Actually, when Laura and Richard's son Luke was born, Anita asked how long they should stay to help. Richard said, "How about kindergarten?" Karen told me she hit the mother-in-law lottery. Greg said he appreciates the joy Anita knew how to bring to life and how excited Logan would be every time Gigi and Papa were coming over. They were always happy to play.

Scott talked about how consistent and present they always were for his daughters and how Scottie learned to be adventurous from Anita and Lucy learned not to let fear lead. Chris told her mother how grateful she is that she showed her how to trust her inner guidance and watch the way she talked to herself. And that she let Chris make her own decisions, even when she would prefer not to! Laura was grateful that with her mother no meant no and yes meant yes. If she agreed to do something, she did it with a full heart, not begrudging resentment. And if she said no—there was no point arguing.

Such precious memories! There is so much that I could share and each of you has stories to tell. I can tell you that Anita was mining her life and learning until the very end. Mike said she felt she was just downloading the wisdom and love directly.

Here are a few whispers of Anita's wisdom:

- look and see the beauty all around you in nature; divine love is there and if you spend time there, you will be restored, enlarged and deepened

- value the water, all the water, because water is life

- stand with those who are standing to protect the water

- respect the wisdom of the elders, especially the indigenous grandmothers who have not forgotten how to live in harmony with the earth

- be silent and listen

- trust what you know in your deepest self—this is where the divine speaks

- your life is sacred
- don't be afraid to speak truth to power
- just because someone has a degree, it doesn't mean they know more than you; knowledge must always serve wisdom.
- show up to your life and stay present
- let your curiosity lead you
- embrace each phase of the journey for it has what you need to learn next
- value the youth who are our future; protect this precious earth for them; teach them they are loved and safe; share your deepest wisdom and learn from their wisdom too
- enjoy life—eat, drink, dance, love, sing, drum, go on adventures, take risks, live fully; when she and Mike were talking about favorite things, Anita said, "One of the things I'm going to miss most is being in a body, I love being in a body!"

Anita McLeod embodied her life as fully as any person I have ever met and we are going to miss her powerful, juicy presence. We are going to miss how she would stand square in front of you and wrap her arms around you and kiss you smack on the lips! But that body no longer served her and she is now free. We mourn and miss the form of our friend. But her essence is so much larger than that. As she neared her death, the doctor asked her, "Are you afraid?" Anita said, "Oh no, oh no, I know where I'm going." Her faith and trust that she would be one with the divine love that had held her all her life was a powerful witness and comfort to her family. I hope it will be a deep comfort to you too. Since her transition through death, many of us have had a very real sense of her presence. Anytime you take a deep breath and tune into your heart or pause to see, hear, smell, taste or touch beauty, you might feel her, right there, loving you, finally One with the divine love that surrounds us all now and forever more. Amen.

REMARKS

Martha Abshire Simmons

Ok, Anita.

Here we are, all these many people you have touched.

All the many people who have had their hearts cracked open by your love.

All these people who know more of who they are because you insisted on knowing yourself without a filter.

Here we are. . . . Our lives are bigger because of your life. Our lives have more life because of your life.

Our tears come more readily.

Our silences are richer.

Our words more precise, more true.

Each of us carry specifically tended pieces of you into our futures, whatever those might be. Each of us has a piece of your song so preciously gifted. Your love is so big.

As it moves through each of us, we are changed, challenged to open to more and more joy, more passion, more knowledge, more humility and more awe.

You've allowed each of us in. You've invited each of us in.

Into a deeper place in our own hearts, and into yours.

It is through this deeper place that more of what life has to say will come through. The light will carry it. Your light will carry it.

And as it does, each of us will be healed of our random hurts, our limitations, our attempts to stay small. There is no smallness in you.

Your unwillingness to settle is an invitation to each of us out here.

Live it. Be it. Allow the light.

Open to the celebration that is your birthright.

We accept, dear Anita.

We accept.

FAMILY REFLECTION OF OUR MOM, DAD'S PARTNER
Scott McLeod

The family has already recognized many familiar and warm faces in attendance today. We thank you for attending this celebration—of our mom, and Dad's partner for the last fifty-five years.

Remember: This *is* a celebration. Do not let our mom down today. She wanted more than anything for this gathering to be three key things:

1st – She wanted everyone to experience beautiful music. She personally selected everything—from the drumming as you entered to the conclusion with "Deep Peace."

2nd – She wanted people from all different backgrounds and experiences and interests to have fellowship together.

She would want each of you—during the reception—to simply find someone that you think is different than yourself —and introduce yourself to them.

Simply ask how they knew Anita and then be open to learn and understand more about that person.

3rd – She wants to see smiles & hear laughter. So let me start with a little humor.

We are pretty confident if Mom had a say for when she would have scheduled this celebration it would have been this upcoming Friday—which coincides with the presidential inauguration.

We can hear her now: "Do it on the twentieth—I can provide the gift of distraction to my friends."

If there was ever one thing that was constant about our mom, it was her desire to always be growing, learning, exploring, getting closer to nature.

Here's a perfect example how she has developed over the years:

When I was in third grade and my brother was in second, we had this wild hair to skip school on a beautiful spring day. So instead of walking to the bus stop to go to Pearsontown Elementary, we walked to a tree house in the woods of our neighborhood.

The first hour was great.

But then a neighbor alerted my mom to the adventure we were having. That neighbor will remain nameless—Barbara Swartz. When we saw Mom walking through the woods to get us—nice dress on and fancy shoes—she was so mad... and probably scared. I mean who skips school when they are in the second grade? High school? Absolutely. Middle school? Maybe. But second grade?

So she dragged our butts into the principal's office where we were severely reprimanded.

It was all Greg's idea, by the way.

But if it had been our recent mom—in her sixties and seventies—who came out to that treehouse that day, after all her lifelong development, after all her experiences, after so much time exploring nature, she would have come up to us and said:

"Wow—this looks like fun. Do you guys have lunch? Can we do this again tomorrow?"

She taught us to always be exploring, always embracing the gifts of nature.

All of us kids would have one-on-one time with Mom over the years—whether it be a scheduled lunch or a cup of coffee or walk on the Duke trail.

We all heard about the different things she was involved in—the women's groups, the Owl Council, the Elder Grandmothers, the workshops through the Resource Center for Women and Ministry in the South that she was either attending or helping to lead.

Admittedly with us kids being in our forties and fifties we did not always "get" it or fully understand it, but we all saw Mom so happy, so excited, so passionate, and it was awesome!!

And we left our one-on-one time with Mom wishing and hoping that when we reach her age we will be just as blessed to have such deep passions and be surrounded by so many wonderful people.

She was a phenomenal role model.

We do wish every one of you could have spent time with our mom between her diagnosis and when her body finally failed.

We believe this was when she was at her finest. Her faith was so strong. She was so full of gratitude, saying over and over, "I have been so blessed."

One night at home after her recent surgery she woke up Dad at three a.m. to tell him she could feel all the love and prayers coming in and it was almost too much for her to take in.

She asked him to hold her and they embraced so he could receive it and share in it.

Always the partner and lover of Dad.

Also during the last several weeks, we heard stories for the first time. For example, she told a story when she returned from a retreat in Moncks Corner, South Carolina, on "befriending death."

She was so moved by what she experienced at the retreat; she approached a few close friends and suggested a similar workshop for Durham. She told the story of how some of her friends were at first hesitant, not sure many people would show up for a workshop called "Befriending Death," but her response was classic. She said, "Really? Really? This happens to all of us . . . and we are not going to talk about it?"

Always the teacher.

Clearly, she left us too soon; most everyone leaves too soon. She could not lessen our sadness or grief but she gave us the priceless gift of comfort. Because we saw her spirit so full of gratitude for her life on this earth and she was confident, ready to embrace her next journey.

REFLECTIONS ON WATER

A RETREAT IN HONOR OF
THE LIFE OF ANITA MCLEOD
AND THE WATERS OF OUR LIVES

September 16, 2017
Timberlake Earth Sanctuary, Whitsett, NC

Nine months after Anita's death a group gathered in nature to commemorate her life, weaving together their appreciation for her and for the waters of the earth that she loved. The event included reflections, prayers, ceremony, a silent "water walk" around the ponds and lake of the earth sanctuary, and communion with it.

In advance of the retreat, participants were asked to

consider the following: "There is a strong sense of Anita's presence, a sense of warm affection, as we anticipate our gathering together. We will honor Water and Anita's life, her courage and commitment to wade into 'Big Waters' in teaching and demonstrating life's most challenging dimensions. This sense is giving us new energies, and we are deeply grateful that we will gather together soon."

REMARKS AT THE RETREAT
Mike McLeod

I want to thank each of you for coming today to be a part of this ritual of blessing the waters and honoring Anita. And a very special thanks to Carolyn and Sherylyn for all the love and work they have put into creating this ceremony.

Anita had dreamed of bringing people together to carry out a ritual of blessing the waters and help raise our awareness of the sacredness of water and that life itself does not exist without water. Anita stood during a meeting on fracking and said, "Water is sacred, we cannot create it and we must protect it."

Even in her short time at Hillcrest, she talked to all of her caretakers about a water blessing ritual and her hopes it would happen in February or March. She gave them the Resource Center website so they could check for dates. Today we gather for this blessing of the waters and to honor Anita.

I think Anita's deep connection to water began when

she spent her summers between five and fifteen years of age playing in the upper Delaware River and the adjoining woods in eastern Pennsylvania. She learned to swim, create playhouses in the rhododendron, and dress up frogs while playing house. The seeds were planted and those experiences affected her in ways that would blossom later in her love for nature and the sacredness of water.

In our married life and in raising our four children we always seemed to end up on the water—from our cabin on Kerr Lake to camping along mountain streams in the Big Horn mountains of Wyoming or sailing on the Pamlico Sound. Anita's favorite time sailing was anchored in South River listening to the herons croaking on the shore, the cries of the osprey circling above us as they looked for their dinner, and if we were fortunate, hearing the blow holes of the porpoises, watching them play as they came up river to feed. The last time we were on the boat in October, we had planned to end up in South River, and Anita said she was going to put out a call to the porpoises since we had not seen them in awhile. Later, after dinner that evening, we were in the cockpit watching the sun go down, and we began to hear the porpoises even before we could see them in the dim light. It was a magical time and of course Anita was very happy.

During Anita's final weeks at home she remembered her Native American name given to her by Ed McGaa, a member of the Oglala Sioux tribe, a spiritual teacher and author of the book, *Mother Earth Spirituality*. In her early fifties,

Anita had attended a retreat led by McGaa, and at the end of the retreat, he signed her copy of the book and gave her the name "Big Waters Woman." He clearly recognized who Anita was and who she was becoming.

Also around the same time, while working for Duke's Health Promotion program, Anita led her first women's circle. The topic was menopause and the importance of women seeing this as a time of transition and potential transformation. For her, menopause was not a medical issue to fear. This experience of gathering women in a circle to share their experiences and their wisdom was life changing for Anita.

I remember her telling me that as she left the circle that day, she had goose bumps running up one side of her body and down the other in recognition of the deep truth of what had happened for her. Returning from the circle that day, she encountered a coworker who said, "Wow! Whatever you have been doing, keep doing it." Later that afternoon, walking up to our house, there on the short walk before the steps was a snakeskin stretched across the walk, clearly a symbol of transformation and shedding. Gathering women in circles to harvest their wisdom became a major purpose in Anita's life.

I quote now from something Anita wrote after her seventieth birthday celebration when many women's circles came together to celebrate her.

"A strong circle is based on a covenant and agreements the members make with one another. In an egalitarian structure, the participants hold the rim of the circle while the center contains the sacred energy where souls can touch The feminine divine is at work in the center of such circles calling us to our deepest and most authentic selves, mending the places of conflict and brokenness and calling forth healing. She calls us to be together in community, to be at home in the world."

It is where we honor the inherent worth and dignity of each other and all life on our earth, life that began in the waters of our planet.

Just two days after Anita's memorial service, our daughter Chris and my sister Melissa had left that morning, and I sat down in the evening for my dinner in the solarium where Anita spent her last weeks. I was alone in the house for the first time. It was very quiet, so I decided to turn on some music, having no idea what CD was in on our CD player. (Anita had used a boom box by her bed for her music, and this CD player had not been used for many months.) As I returned to the table, I began to hear the sound of dripping water coming from the speakers and then gradually the sound of water over stones like a mountain brook, and then the sound of the surf. I had never heard this CD before. When I finally looked up from the table, I saw a full moon filling a high small window in the solarium. The timing, the synchronicity of water sounds, and rising moon led to a deep sense of awe and connection to Anita.

At the end of her poem "At the River Clarion," Mary Oliver says,

And still, pressed deep into my mind, the river
keeps coming, touching me, passing by on its
long journey, its pale, infallible voice
singing.[11]

REMARKS

~~~~~~~~~~~~~~~~~~~~~~~~~~~~~~~

Dinner Celebration on the Occasion of Anita's Birthday
November 29, 2017

Mike McLeod

[NOTE: On the first anniversary of Anita's death a group
of her family and friends gathered in remembrance and celebration of her life, an event called "Circles of Gratitude,"
circles connected with the Resource Center and especially
circles of those who gathered with Anita. These are the remarks shared by her husband, Mike, on that occasion.]

INTRODUCTION: I want to thank Jeanette and the
Resource Center for Women and Ministry in the South
for this gathering tonight to honor Anita and her legacy of
women's circles. It is my intention to support the Resource
Center in continuing her work around conscious aging and
intergenerational circles.

   This would have been Anita's 78th birthday, and she had
said to me during her brief illness that she knew her 77th

would be "big" but she had no idea it would involve this journey. It has been a heartbreaking journey for me and yet as I go day by day through this grief, I have brief glimpses of joy and gratitude for the life we had together and all I learned from Anita. Whatever I say in the next few minutes are my responsibility and I do not pretend to say what Anita would say at this moment. As each of you know, she would have clear and strong opinions on these topics.

Anita felt circles allowed the creation of a safe container where women could share their experiences and be received and affirmed in the circle, and in doing this could discover their own truth, could listen to their own inner source of wisdom. For Anita, circles involved vulnerability and the courage to discover who we are meant to be in the face of a culture that promotes living on the surface of life. She felt circles generated an energy that could be given to the center of the circle or taken from the center to the individual, depending on needs. Circles also led to a sense of belonging.

As most of you know, her first groups centered on menopause as a natural transition and potential for transformation. It was not a medical issue.

Entering her 60s she was looking for "the road maps"—going on a vision quest in southwestern Colorado, gathering groups around the topic of conscious aging—ways to be fully awake to all we are, healing wounds around regrets and forgiveness. Ways to learn what parts of ourselves we left behind growing up in our families and culture, crucial parts, like assertiveness, enthusiasm, creativity, and sensuality.

Later, Anita was involved in end-of-life issues. She led intergenerational workshops like Heron's Walk that involved women's circles in nature, and later helped to lead intergenerational writing groups.

A second focus for Anita was the sacredness of nature, including the waters, and she went to the woods often to be restored and to seek answers to her questions. As Rilke said to the young poet, "Love the questions", "Live the questions." I would say, living with Anita for fifty-five years, that she lived her questions.

A third and final emphasis was the importance of courage. We had many conversations over the years around fear and our desire to frame it as our growing edge, to face our uncertainty and walk the path.

Anita combined curiosity and courage. Courage to go on a vision quest in her early sixties. Courage to choose open brain surgery to remove the cancer while she was awake communicating with the surgeon rather than just biopsy and radiation alone. She had been told patients in her age group were usually given a more conservative treatment. After thinking about her choices overnight, she asked Lucy, our granddaughter, to go on a walk with her on the ward, telling her she would not let fear be her guide and would choose open surgery. Courage was there when we met with the radiation oncologist midway through her treatment. Despite what at first looked like excellent surgical results, her cancer rapidly reoccurred. At this point Anita was paralyzed on her left side and had said to me she could not envision going forward in a life where she could not walk in the woods, be on the boat or be part of her women's circles. She told the radiation oncologist she was stopping the treatment, not wanting to risk any loss of her mental function for whatever time that remained.

I will never forget what Anita said the first day after surgery, surrounded by our family, "This journey is about love and not just about me."

The circles that will continue to gather through the efforts of the Resource Center are in their essence about love and the courage to open our hearts, about letting down our protective walls and willing to be vulnerable. Loving involves vulnerability and as poet David Whyte says:

> I want to know if you are willing to live, day by day, with the consequence of love and the bitter unwanted passion of sure defeat.[12]

The late anthropologist, Angeles Arrien, borrowed four principles from the indigenous cultures she studied. I feel Anita lived these principles, planting her seeds of wisdom:

1. Show up and be present . . .
2. Pay attention to what has heart and meaning. . . .
3. Tell the truth without blame or judgment. . . .
4. Be open to outcome, not attached to outcome.[13]

I thank each of you for coming tonight. I want to close with a few lines from Pema Chödrön:

This continual ache of the heart
is a blessing that when accepted fully
can be shared with all.[14]

OBITUARY

Anita McLeod (1939–2017)

Anita Marion Swensen McLeod passed peacefully on Monday, January 9, less than eight weeks after being diagnosed with a malignant brain tumor. Just as she lived, Anita died on her own terms, in her own home, teaching us every step of the way.

Anita grew up in Ridgefield, New Jersey, the daughter of Catherine and Arne Swensen and sister to Paul Swensen. She ventured south to attend Duke University, graduating with a B.S. in Nursing. She met Mike McLeod, a doctor at Duke Hospital, when they were caring for the same patient, and married him three weeks after graduation.

Anita and Mike raised their four children in Durham, years before it was a hip and happening place. In 1974, the couple embarked on a sabbatical during which they camped across the country (with all four kids in a pop-up camper) and then lived in Marin County, California, for a year to explore living out west. While they ultimately returned to Durham, their time in California forever changed the family in deep and meaningful ways. Years later, their children still footnote family stories and any references to their parents with "BC" (Before California) and "AC" (After California).

After returning from California, Anita decided to go back to work to renew her nursing license. Before doing so, she made sure all her children learned how to cook and do their own laundry, a reflection of her commitment to raise independent, self-sufficient children, unaware that it would be these qualities that would forever endear her to her future daughters-in-law.

After working with Jeanette Stokes in a class on women's spirituality, Anita became more involved with the Resource Center for Women in Ministry in the South, eventually serving as the organization's Board Chair. She was a connector and convener of sacred circles where women shared and honored each other's wisdom. She used her passion for teaching to facilitate workshops on such varied topics as menopause, conscious aging, and befriending death. She was deeply committed to promoting intergenerational conversations with the hope that universal feminine values could be brought into society to help create a more caring world. Anita founded the RCWMS Elder Women's Spirituality Project to encourage elder women's spiritual and creative development and their ongoing engagement in the world.

Wife, mother, grandmother, friend, teacher, convener and lover of the natural world, Anita embraced each of her roles equally, enriching the lives of all who had the privilege of knowing her. If you were fortunate enough to be Anita's friend, you knew the meaning of fierce compassion and the power of deep listening. If you were lucky enough to have Anita as a teacher, your life might just be changed forever. If you were one of her children or grandchildren, you were blessed to know unconditional love and understand how her high expectations inspired you to follow your dreams.

Anita's 55-year partnership with Mike McLeod reflected her deep commitment to her family and to living an intentional life. She was a relentless seeker of truth, a voracious reader, a lover of beauty, a devoted friend, and deeply aware of how fortunate she was to find a partner who shared so many of her passions. Anita was beloved for her resilient spirit, fierce compassion, relentless optimism, insatiable curiosity and keen sense of humor, and was also known to be graciously stubborn on occasion.

For over thirty years, Anita and Mike enjoyed sailing their boat, "Free to Be" on their beloved Pamlico Sound, taking turns serving as captain. They also loved camping in Montana and Wyoming. It was a testament to their partnership that even after 55 years of marriage, Anita and Mike still enjoyed spending time together in small, cramped spaces.

Anita is survived by her husband, Mike McLeod (Durham) and her four children Chris McLeod (Charlotte), Scott McLeod and wife Missy (Durham) and Greg McLeod and wife Karen (Raleigh) and Laura McLeod and husband Richard Moberly (Lincoln, NE) and five grandchildren: Scottie, Lucy, and Logan McLeod, and Luke and Henry Moberly. She was predeceased by her brother, Paul Swensen.

The family would like to express their profound gratitude to Acorn Home Care and Anita's caregivers, Tammy Bobbit, Meikio Spring and Sally-Irene Ngeve as well as the physicians and nurses at Duke Cancer Center.

After a family graveside service, a service celebrating the life of Anita McLeod will be convened by Reverend Debra Brazzel on Monday, January 16, 2017 at Eno River Unitarian Universalist Fellowship, 4907 Garrett Road, Durham, NC. Friends are invited to visit with the family immediately following the service.

In lieu of flowers, the McLeod family invites you to consider a memorial gift to one of the following charities: RCWMS (Resource Center for Women in Ministry in the South), 1202 Watts Street, Durham NC 27701; Timberlake Earth Sanctuary, 1501 Rock Creek Dairy Road, Whitsett NC 27377; or Eno River Association, 4404 Guess Road, Durham NC 27712.

Hall-Wynne is handling funeral arrangements.

APPENDIX B

WORKSHOPS, EVENTS, AND RETREATS

Anita created, facilitated, and participated in a rich variety of programs, workshops, and retreats for the Elder Women's Spirituality Project. Where noted, a few of the workshops in the Elder Women's Spirituality Project were led by others.

February 6–March 13, 2001 (Tuesdays)
Duke Continuing Education, Durham, NC
EXPLORING WOMEN'S SPIRITUALITY:
A JOURNEY TO WHOLENESS
Explore your experience of the sacred with other women. Journey into such areas as images of the feminine divine, the mind/body/spirit connection, creativity, life transitions, and grace. We'll make use of journaling, silence, music, art, poetry, and small group discussions.
LEADERS: Anita McLeod and Jeanette Stokes

February 5–March 12, 2002 (Tuesdays)
Duke Continuing Education, Durham, NC
EXPLORING WOMEN'S SPIRITUALITY:
A JOURNEY TO WHOLENESS
LEADERS: Anita McLeod and Jeanette Stokes

March 15–16, 2002
MOTHERS & DAUGHTERS: EXPLORING THE GRANDMOTHER/MOTHER/DAUGHTER RELATIONSHIP
East Duke Building, Duke University, Durham, NC
How often do you hear a woman say, "My worst fear as I get older is of becoming my mother"? And yet, the relationship between mother and daughter is the context in which our feelings about ourselves and the possibilities for our lives as women are formed. This retreat will provide an opportunity for women to sift through the gifts and challenges of this crucial relationship.
LEADERS: Miriam Biber, Anita McLeod, Chris McLeod, Jeanette Stokes, Hollister Trott, and Rachael Wooten

January 25, 2003
WISDOM & MENOPAUSE
East Duke Building, Duke University, Durham, NC
Menopause is a deeply meaningful threshold in a woman's life. The first half of life is often outer-directed, a time when we put the needs of others before our own. Menopause can mark a transition to a more balanced time, when we turn inward and define for ourselves how we want to live. Our culture values youth and devalues older women. Menopause has been depicted as a problem to be solved with drugs. In this workshop, we will approach this threshold with honor and respect, challenge the cultural beliefs in a supportive group, gain information, and listen to each other's stories. Together

we will discover the profound wisdom imbedded in this life process. We will make use of journaling, silence, relaxation, poetry, music, and small group discussions.
LEADER: Anita McLeod

February 4–March 11, 2003
Duke Continuing Education, Durham, NC
EXPLORING WOMEN'S SPIRITUALITY:
A JOURNEY TO WHOLENESS
LEADERS: Anita McLeod and Jeanette Stokes

January 24, 2004
WISDOM & MENOPAUSE
East Duke Building, Duke University, Durham, NC
LEADER: Anita McLeod

April 23, 2005
WOMEN OVER SIXTY
Durham, NC
Thousands of women whose lives and attitudes have been shaped by the Women's Movement are now entering their sixties. Never before in recorded history have there been so many women of age with so much competence, experience, independence, and resourcefulness. Still, many of us find ourselves asking, "What now? What's next?" It is time to usher in a new round of consciousness-raising, time to challenge the negative stereotypes of older women and revive the wise woman within. In this workshop, we will chal-

lenge cultural stereotypes in a supportive atmosphere, gain information, and listen to one another. We will use journaling, silence, poetry, humor, and small group discussions. Together we will discover the profound wisdom imbedded in our life experiences.

LEADER: Anita McLeod

September 12, October 10, November 7, & December 5, 2005
WOMEN OVER SIXTY WRITING GROUP
Durham, NC

As we enter our sixties, many of us desire to explore the possibilities of this stage of life: How do I speak my truth? What are some of the most valuable life lessons I've learned so far? What part of my life is still unlived? Come join a circle of women over sixty who will use writing as a tool to till the soil of our awareness, plant seeds for the future, harvest our life experiences, and share what we are learning about ourselves. Using silence as a way of centering ourselves and writing exercises to spark our imaginations, we will create a safe environment for writing and reading to each other during class time. No formal writing experience is required.

LEADERS: Anita McLeod and Margie Hattori

October 27–28, 2006
WOMEN OVER SIXTY
Durham, NC
Spend Friday evening and Saturday in a circle of women over sixty as we create a new vision of ourselves as elder women. We will learn from each other as we speak of our experiences of aging, share our challenges and longings, and harvest our valuable life lessons. Together we will name future possibilities that we haven't yet imagined.
LEADERS: Anita McLeod and Margie Hattori

October 4–7, 2007
WISE CHOICES (formerly Women Over Sixty)
Pelican House, Trinity Center, Pine Knoll Shores, NC
LEADERS: Anita McLeod and Margie Hattori

March 15, 2008
THE GIFTS OF MENOPAUSE
Durham, NC
Menopause can be a profoundly meaningful journey in a woman's life as she responds to the wisdom of her body and consults her inner knowing. It is a time when she is called to listen deeply to herself. The first half of a woman's life is outer-directed, a time when she puts the needs of others before her own. Responding to menopause as an invitation to listen to her soul can bring rich gifts from her inner well-spring. As a woman makes her way through this passage,

the quality of her experience is affected by the state of her health, her approach to change, her beliefs about menopause, her ability to nurture and listen to herself, and her network of support.
LEADER: Anita McLeod

February 27, 2010
WOMEN'S SOULFUL CIRCLES
Durham, NC

For thousands of years, women have gathered in circles to share their lives, to support and learn from one other. Sitting together and sharing the stories of our lives deepens our relationships with others and with ourselves. As we speak what is true, we develop our authentic voices. As we listen carefully to others, we become more compassionate. Within the safety of a structured circle format, you will learn the basic practices of council sharing. The participants form the rim of a circle whose center holds sacred energy. Come to experience a safe women's circle and learn how to create your own nurturing community.
LEADER: Anita McLeod

April 29, 2012
LEGACY PLANNING FOR WOMEN
Durham, NC

There comes a time in your life when you long to know that your life somehow has purpose. You seek to leave a meaningful mark on the world. Legacy Planning can help you discover ways to use the resources and experiences you've accumulated in life to make a lasting impression on those you love and the causes you believe in.

LEADER: Lisa Gabriel, certified financial planner

MAY 25–JUNE 3, 2012
THEORY AND PRACTICE OF THE WORK THAT RECONNECTS
stone circles, The Stone House, Mebane, NC
Bring forth fresh vision, courage, and creativity in this time of planetary crisis.

LEADER: Eco-philosopher Joanna Macy

September 8, 2012
HARVESTING OUR STORIES: COLLECTING OUR WISDOM
The autumn of our lives is the time for harvesting the wisdom of our lives. As we enter our later years, it is important to unearth and gather up our life stories, to share them with others, to reflect on what we have learned by experience, and to discern how we might want to pass on our wisdom. This workshop is designed for women 55 and older. As a follow-up, we will offer an optional monthly morning writing circle for those who attend the workshop and who would like to continue to harvest their stories.

LEADERS: Anita McLeod and Liz Dowling-Sendor

September 22, 2012
"WHEN GRANDMOTHERS SPEAK, THE EARTH WILL HEAL" (from a Hopi saying)
Timberlake Earth Sanctuary, Whitsett, NC
It has been well said that in today's technological world, grandmothers have a special role to fulfill in sharing their love of the natural world with succeeding genera tions. Come and enjoy a quiet day spent at nature's pace surrounded by beauty and learn some special ways of sharing a love of the earth with grandchildren and all children.
LEADERS: Carolyn Toben and Anita McLeod

October 27, 2012
GIVING THANKS TO THE EARTH
New Hope Camp & Conference Center, Chapel Hill, NC
We are living in a perilous time: our water, soil, air, and all living beings on earth are in jeopardy. Many people are trapped in despair and inaction, but despair is not the only option. Come join with others who want to find another way. Tap into your creative imagination and experience an introduction to Joanna Macy's vision of "Active Hope" in a beautiful natural setting. Join us as we enliven our connection to the natural world, express our gratitude to mother earth, resonate with her suffering, and consider how we can support her. We'll engage in personal writing, conversation, simple drawing, and basic movement to live music. Together we will create a community of creative expres-

sion that will inspire us to help heal and protect the earth. Previous experience or skill in movement or drawing is not expected or needed.

LEADER: Ann Simon Koppelman, semi-retired clinical psychologist

November 27, 2012
READING BY CAROLYN TOBEN
Durham, NC
Carolyn Toben spent many hours over ten years with renowned priest, author, and cultural historian Thomas Berry, engaged in deep discussions about his foundational thinking on the human-earth-Divine relationship. She will read from her book about the experience, *Recovering a Sense of the Sacred: Conversations with Thomas Berry*

December 1, 2012
A DAY OF QUIET
King's Daughters Inn, Durham, NC
The gentle gifts of winter can be lost in the frantic swirl of the holiday season. Instead of being a time of quiet reflection, December can become a time of disconnection from ourselves and from the earth. Periods of silence and solitude may help us notice the diminished light and appreciate the beauty of a world laid bare for a time. Drawing inward and being quiet may help us truly connect in community. Join us for a time of remembering our tender yearnings for

peace, hope, love, and joy. Together we will explore ways of deepening our connection to the sacred by opening our breathing and meditation. The afternoon will include silent time together, an exploration of lovingkindness, walking softly outside, and a simple art reflection. No meditation experience required.

LEADERS: Barbara Anderson, Associate Director, African Studies Center, UNC, and Anita McLeod

January 27, February 10, February 24, March 10, & March 17, 2013

END-OF-LIFE SERIES

Durham, NC in a comfortable private home with a cat This multi-part series offers resources, information, and exploration of issues facing all of us as we prepare for the end of our life. Join a circle of courageous women willing to explore what a "good death" might mean and how preparing for it opens us to wholeheartedly embrace the precious life that awaits us.

LEADERS: Anita McLeod; Betsy Barton, Duke Medical Center; Carolyn H. Burrus, Hospice Chaplain and Bereavement Counselor; Sharon Thompson, attorney; Lisa Gabriel, financial planner; and Anne Watson Davis, attorney.

April 19–21, 2013
OUR NATURE, IN NATURE: A WOMEN'S RETREAT
Timberlake Earth Sanctuary, Whitsett, NC (near Greensboro)
In the spring we are called to be outside, relishing earth's
warm winds, colorful blooms, and blue skies. The natural
world, mirror of our own nature, invites us to nurture, empower, and transform ourselves. Indigenous cultures knew
the sacredness of the natural world, its seasons, and its
compass directions. Together we will explore the wisdom of
each direction as it pertains to our current life situations. As
we establish a safe community together for this weekend,
we will spend time in Council practice and alone time on
the land to experience its messages for us. Camping is an
option. Elder women and younger women will learn from
and inspire one another.
LEADERS: Pat Webster, clinical psychologist, and Anita
McLeod

September 7, 2013
THE ART OF AGING: CELEBRATING ELDERHOOD
Colony Hills Clubhouse, 3060 Colony Road, Durham NC
Join a circle of women as we explore our experience of
aging and discover ways to embrace the opportunities and
challenges of this rich time of life. Contemplate awakening
to the adventure of conscious aging and the many possible
gifts of enlivenment.
LEADERS: Lyndall Hare, gerontologist, and Anita McLeod

September 22, 2013
CONSIDER THE CONVERSATION: FILM &
DISCUSSION
Watts Street Baptist Church, Durham, NC
When longtime friends Terry Kaldhusdal, a fourth-grade
teacher and filmmaker, and Michael Bernhagen, a healthcare business professional turned hospice advocate, each
lost loved ones to chronic disease, their experiences led
them to produce a documentary that would inspire change
in end-of-life care that is more person-centered and less
system-centered.
LEADERS: Betsy Barton

October 12, 2013
HARVESTING OUR STORIES: COLLECTING OUR
WISDOM
Durham, NC
The autumn of our lives is a time to harvest the wisdom of
our lives, to unearth and gather up our life stories, to share
them with others, to reflect on what we have learned by ex-
perience, and to discern how we might pass on our wisdom.
For women 55 and older.
LEADERS: Liz Dowling-Sendor and Anita McLeod

October 19, 2013
COUNCIL OF ALL BEINGS
New Hope Camp & Conference Center, Chapel Hill, NC

A chance for people to experience their connection with the natural world by speaking in the voice of an endangered being, such as a plant, an animal, a rock, etc.
LEADERS: Ann Simon Koppelman and Anita McLeod

October 27, 2013
WOMEN & MONEY
Durham, NC
Everyone has a personal money journey. What confusing messages did you receive in childhood about money? Do you harbor feelings around such issues as abundance, scarcity, earning, investing, spending and giving? How do these messages and feelings intersect with your core values and/or spiritual beliefs? Join a circle of women as we explore ways to align our financial actions with our values.
LEADERS: Lisa Gabriel, financial planner, and Anita McLeod

November 9, 2013
HARVESTING OUR STORIES: COLLECTING OUR WISDOM
Colony Hills Clubhouse, Durham NC
LEADERS: Anita McLeod and Liz Dowling-Sendor

December 8, 2013
A DAY OF QUIET
King's Daughters Inn, Durham, NC
LEADERS: Barbara Anderson and Anita McLeod

April 8, 2014, 9:30 a.m.–4:00 p.m.
"WHEN GRANDMOTHERS SPEAK, THE EARTH
WILL HEAL" (from a Hopi saying)
Timberlake Farm, Whitsett, NC
Inspired by the International Council of 13 Indigenous
Grandmothers, this retreat explores ways to bridge the
separation between humans and the natural world. Will
include meditation, shared stories, and silent walks on
wooded trails. Please bring a bag lunch.
LEADERS: Carolyn Toben, founder of the Center for
Education, Imagination, and the Natural World at
Timberlake Farm Earth Sanctuary, and Anita McLeod

April 16, 2014
CONSIDER THE CONVERSATION: FILM &
DISCUSSION
Durham County Main Library
LEADER: Betsy Barton

October 23–26, 2014 (7 p.m. Thursday–3 p.m. Sunday)
HERON'S WALK ON WATER'S EDGE, A RETREAT
Cedar Cross Retreat Center, Louisburg NC (north of
Raleigh)
She walks along the water's wooded edge. Her steps inten-
tional. Heron stands, knowing wisdom is rooted in intuition,
imagination, and bodily sensations. Her observation is keen.
During this intergenerational retreat, we will return to our
natural pace and draw closer to Sacred Mystery embodied in

the earth community. We will find the Divine in our own reflections, in each other and in "all of our relations." Through soul circles and eco-contemplative practices, we will open to the most relevant reciprocal healing medicine of our time, intimate relationship with the natural world.

LEADERS: Sherylyn Pitt and Anita McLeod

January 18, February 15, & March 8, 2015 (3 Sunday afternoons)

BEFRIENDING DEATH

This series will invite participants to contemplate death, consider practices that might help them be present to themselves and others in the experience of dying, and reflect on ways to deepen their appreciation of life.

LEADERS: Betsy Barton, Stacy Grove, Anita McLeod, and Jocelyn Streid

July 26, August 23, & September 20, 2015, Sundays

CONSCIOUS ELDERING: GOING DEEPER SERIES

In a comfortable home in Durham with a cat

Three-part series on the powerful inner work of creating an elderhood rich in meaning, passion and wisdom.

7/26 Life Review: Legacy of Our Stories with Anita McLeod and Sherylyn Pitt

8/23 Compassion, Forgiveness and Letting Go with Linda Barnett and Sherylyn Pitt

9/20 Finding Passion and Purpose with Stacy Grove and Sherylyn Pitt

October 1–4, 2015
HERON'S WALK ON WATER'S EDGE, A RETREAT
LEADERS: Sherylyn Pitt and Anita McLeod

October 26–November 16, 2015 (4 Mondays)
TURNING POINTS: INTERGENERATIONAL
WRITING WORKSHOP
Together we will explore life turning points, using writing
as a spiritual and self-revelatory practice. We will reflect on
ancient images of the Maiden/Mother/Crone archetype,
while also finding new ways of envisioning our unique and
universal spiraling journeys through life.
LEADERS: Anita McLeod and Rebecca Welper

January 17, February 14, & March 13, 2016 (3 Sunday
afternoons)
BEFRIENDING DEATH
LEADERS: Betsy Barton, Jehanne Gheith, Stacy Grove,
and Anita McLeod

Second Tuesday of the month (began in October 2013 and
continues in 2019)
THE ART OF CONSCIOUS AGING: AN ONGOING
GROUP
Colony Hills Clubhouse, Durham NC
Participants will create a sacred container for reflection in
community on the art of conscious aging. Each gathering

will focus on a single topic. Participants will have an opportunity to provide program leadership. Any woman who experiences herself at any stage of her elder years is invited to join us in a deep sharing of her own experiences.

ENDNOTES

1. Mary Oliver, "The Summer Day," *New and Selected Poems: Volume One* (Boston: Beacon Press, 1992), 94.

2. Oliver, 94.

3. Oliver, 94.

4. Oliver, 94.

5. Center for Action and Contemplation, "The Natural World: Week 2, The Great Turning" https://cac.org/the-great-turning-2018-03-14/.

6. Maxine Kumin, "The Archeology of a Marriage," *Poetry*, April 1978, 3.

7. Oliver, 94.

8. Oliver, 94.

9. Mary Oliver, "When Death Comes," *New and Selected Poems: Volume One* (Boston: Beacon Press, 1992), 10.

10. Kahlil Gibran, "The Beauty of Death," *A Tear and a Smile* (New York: Alfred A. Knopf, 1950), 172.

11. Mary Oliver, "At the River Clarion," *Evidence* (Boston: Beacon Press, 2010), 51.

12. David Whyte, "Self Portrait," from *Fire in the Earth* (Vancouver: Many Rivers, Press, 1992), 10.

13. Angeles Arrien, *The Four-Fold Way* (New York: Harper Collins, 1993), 7-8.

14. Pema Chödrön, *The Places that Scare You: A Guide to Fearlessness in Difficult Times*, (Boston: Shambhala, 2002), p. 4.